TOURBILLON
INTERNATIONAL

THE NEW
MODERN MEDIA

Remaking Media for a Mobile Culture

Lew Dickey

TOURBILLON
INTERNATIONAL

New York   Los Angeles   Chicago

TOURBILLON INTERNATIONAL

261 Madison Ave., 3rd Floor, New York, NY 10016, U.S.A.
10250 Constellation Blvd., Ste. 2710, Los Angeles, CA 90067, U.S.A.
33 W. Monroe Street, Ste. 2100, Chicago, IL 60603, U.S.A.

Tourbillon International books are available at special discounts for bulk purchases
for sales promotions or corporate use. Special editions, including personalized covers,
excerpts of existing books, or books with corporate logo, can be created in large quantities
for special needs. For more information, contact Sean Bertram at (312) 274-2547.

PRINTED IN THE UNITED STATES OF AMERICA

Book and cover design by Gregory Odendahl

10 9 8 7 6 5 4 3 2 1
First Edition

For my mother, Patricia, and my wife, Vanessa.

CONTENTS

INTRODUCTION

Writing this book has been an exciting journey that drew heavily from more than 30 years of media experience as an entrepreneur and executive, as well as being a passionate student of both the media and technology industries. As a Founder/CEO and builder of Cumulus Media from a pure start-up into the nation's second largest radio company, as well as co-founding and building the nation's largest regional magazine publishing business, I've witnessed the halcyon days of traditional media pre-digital & mobile, as well as the difficult transition into the current environment where content distribution and monetization are being significantly disrupted at an accelerating pace. I was reminded of the famous counterculture meme from the '60s espousing, "The revolution will not be televised." Today, it would include the rejoinder, "but it will be streamed." The cultural revolution of the '60s has been replaced by the digital revolution of the 21st century, which is profoundly disrupting every legacy media and advertising business.

In my many discussions over the past couple of years with friends and colleagues throughout the media and advertising business, it was clear that people are aware of the changes underfoot, but due to day-to-day demands and operational pressures of "hitting their numbers," few have the time to reflect on the profound changes that will render several existing business models obsolete as early as 2020. Lack of perspective is the primary reason why the business land-scape is littered with companies—as well as entire industries—that fail to embrace both trends and technology that lead to fundamental change in consumer demand, product innovation and distribution. For example, retailers have largely missed the trend toward online shopping, paving the way for Amazon and others to gain critical mass and materially disrupt their models. Similarly, television networks and pay TV distributors have witnessed the growth of Net-flix, which now boasts more than twice as many subscribers in the U.S. than either Comcast or DirecTV—the two largest pay TV distributors.

This book is a useful text to provide perspective and analytical frameworks to help people think through the important trends which will shape the future of media and advertising and the competitiveness of the companies which produce, distribute and monetize media and advertising content. Change is accelerating and will continue to bring both volatility and opportunity for the entire media and advertising ecosystem including incumbents, start-ups, industry professionals, investors and consumers.

Regardless of the structural impediment—regulatory or capital, print and electronic media businesses successfully leveraged high barriers to entry which served to limit competition and thus, sustained an attractive industry structure for more than a half century. However, technology is now impacting media in more profound ways than perhaps any other industry with the exception of the tech industry itself. The internet and mobile devices have become the catalysts for the profound changes in how society interacts, works, consumes media, banks, shops and manages daily activities. The fundamental behavioral change that has occurred since the launch of the iPhone is demonstrably greater than the cumulative change in the 25 years before it. Moreover, the rate of change and disruption continues to accelerate.

To better understand the seminal shifts driving these changes, it first requires a cogent analysis of the effects of technology on consumer behavior and across the media industry. This analysis requires a strategic framework for how media businesses will need to evolve in order to leverage their core strengths in content creation against the very strong gravitational forces driving disaggregation through digital distribution; and serves as the catalyst for unprecedented industry change with the fortunes of many companies and industry outcomes over the next decade uncertain at best. A forward-thinking, non-defensive and genuinely proactive approach to strategic planning is now more important than ever before. I'm hopeful that people will find useful frameworks and valuable context in these pages to help them better understand the powerful forces which are upending the status quo, for as the apocryphal saying goes, "may we live in interesting times."

1 | LOOKING THROUGH THE PRISM
OF THE NEW MODERN MEDIA

The new era of Modern Media represents one of the most exciting times in the storied history of media, but it also promises to be a period of immense uncertainty as primacy is reordered while a new industry structure takes shape. Traditional and New Media are well along on the path to convergence as content creators become ever more empowered through the democratization of digital distribution platforms. Content is now more abundant, more accessible and more affordable—a trend which will continue for the foreseeable future. Modern media companies will be more vertically integrated across multiple platforms and structured against "audiences" like Millennials rather than "mediums" such as newspapers, TV stations, cable networks, magazines or radio stations. Multiplatform brands that speak directly to audiences will eclipse general purpose networks or channels as medium agnostic consumers gravitate towards compelling content and brands delivered through their most convenient device(s) at the moment they choose to consume it.

Predicting the next five or 10 years in either media or technology is always difficult, but emerging trends and themes explored throughout this book are the operative truths that will influence media's accelerating transformation into the next decade and beyond. The new era of Modern Media will result from the logical convergence of traditional and new media and will serve to democratize content creation, transform content distribution through scaled digital platforms and create reimagined business models adapting to tech-enabled market efficiency for content and advertising.

PRISM: THE FIVE KEY THEMES OF MODERN MEDIA

Figuratively, a prism provides a distinct point of view for clarifying complex subject matter so it serves as both an appropriate and intuitive acronym for the comprehensive framework that defines the five pillars of Modern Media. These key themes will inform the ultimate transformation of the media business' existing industry structure into the new modern landscape.

- **P**ersonalization: Content will be individualized and consumed on demand
- **R**esponsive: Advertising will speak to an audience of one
- **I**nteractive: Content will be distributed to all screens over IP
- **S**ubscription: Fee-based offerings will become an essential revenue stream
- **M**ultiplatform: Leading brands will be device-agnostic

The five **PRISM** themes defining Modern Media will drive the competitive strategies of both traditional and digital media companies. These five seminal tenets will profoundly impact the ultimate re-ordering of the media and advertising business as the legacy and new media ecosystems converge into a new structure which optimizes the strengths of each and sunsets companies which are unable to adapt.

PERSONALIZATION IS TABLE STAKES IN THE MODERN MEDIA ECOSYSTEM

Viewed from a more holistic perspective, the collective effect of internet search, social media, mobile apps and messaging platforms have forever altered behavioral norms, materially changing consumer attitudes and expectations with respect to media and commerce. Consumers are now King (or Queen) and have been conditioned to expect their media and commerce experiences to be on their terms versus the legacy, pre-mobile days when media was mostly linear, prices were higher, choices were fewer and the burdens of inconvenience were routinely borne by consumers.

Today's mobile-centric consumer is largely in control of their media and entertainment experiences, which increasingly include consuming their content on demand. Consumer behavior is becoming a series of discrete, micro-moments where more impulsive decisions and consumption patterns are exhibited due to the freedom and flexibility of mobile connectivity. IP distribution facilitates the individual addressability for both content and advertising, which is leading to a more engaging experience for consumers who increasingly demand more personalized and convenient offerings in their daily lives.

Internet of Things (IoT) technology enables virtually every piece of media content ever produced to be individually accessed by every connected device on the planet. Furthermore, cloud-based storage and computing will enable a seamless user experience as modern media companies will increasingly leverage IoT technology with an intuitive user interface to create a highly personalized media experience to meet the needs of diverse and demanding consumers. Going forward, successful media companies will be highly-personalized and monetize premium content across multiple distribution platforms and sales channels.

In the next decade, consumers will routinely create their own newspaper, their own television experience and their own radio stations in a single content offering of video, audio and text just as they customize newsfeeds on their social networks today. Premium content will continue to be in high demand, but branded distribution that is not well-defined, targeted and extended across multiple platforms will become increasingly diluted and simply fade into irrelevance.

Telltale signs for troubled models include newspapers filled with wire service content, television stations without a strong local news presence, radio stations that are music intensive jukeboxes or heavy on non-local content, cable networks heavy on non-exclusive or poorly rated content and record labels who simply offer their artists radio promotion and rev share deals from third-party digital distributors. These competitive strategies and business models are all at risk of being diluted and diminished by the emerging Modern Media ecosystem.

People are now able to consume media content as episodic and on demand; and therefore increasingly eschew appointment viewing in favor of engaging with a piece of content when they're in the mood. It's a wonderful opportunity for media companies and consumer brands to interact with more consumers at multiple points throughout the day and week, but it requires incremental new content strategies and ad formats to remain relevant and authentic with a consistent brand ethos.

Developing compelling brands that resonate with well-defined communities of interest will serve as the requisite packaging around the multimedia content and experiential offerings for both consumers and marketers. In a world where virtually every piece of content will be available on demand, developing a compelling brand with an integrated content experience across multiple platforms is the most effective way to positively differentiate the offering for consumers and de-commoditize the companion ad products for sponsors.

Leading the way in the trend towards personalization will be marketers in search of higher ROI through data-driven targeting, programmatic buying, real-time bidding and dynamic advertising. Embracing technology is now a strategic imperative that media and marketing executives ignore at their peril as historic transformations like mobile, social, messaging and ad tech have a tendency to be ignored by the disrupted until the tipping point is reached as evidenced by both newspapers and record labels.

RESPONSIVE AD TECHNOLOGY PROMISES HIGHER ROI

As we look to the future of media, it is most instructive to understand how digital technology has evolved to provide the context for the ongoing disruption that will ultimately evolve the traditional media business into the new modern paradigm. The digital media ecosystem began to take root with the commercialization of internet search engines as Google and others organized the vast amount of information on the web. It made the internet suddenly accessible to almost everyone, catalyzing a virtuous circle for what would become the world's largest information network. Search also began the trend of data-driven marketing as advertisers bid for key words to optimize their chances of discovery through search and were required to pay only when a prospect "clicked" or engaged with their message.

Search and innovative ad technology enabled Google to build a near $100 billion global advertising business by first revolutionizing the way people accessed information and then adroitly creating a business model to productize and sell a new form of advertising to millions of marketers. Data-driven targeting and interactive advertising developed through search also served as the foundation for another incredible business model we know as social media. Like Google did several years before them with search, Facebook commercialized and dominated the next transformational trend in the shift to online media and advertising with dominance in social media.

Search became the mass adoption application that met a need for utility, but social media quickly became the "killer" app that profoundly changed society. Social media created an entirely new use case for consumers to connect, communicate and share—and they quickly became addicted. Facebook claims over 1.8 billion active users with the majority of Americans regularly using Facebook or their sister network, Instagram. The popularity of Facebook, Instagram, Snapchat and Twitter has spawned hundreds of social networks and messaging apps for both the consumer and enterprise markets, and, as people continue to share more and more information through scaled digital platforms, it creates additional opportunities to collect vast amounts of user data.

The volume of data now being captured on individual consumers through their online activities is unprecedented, providing valuable information to marketers on both identity and intent. This trove of data is driving the rapidly evolving ad technology space and enabling marketers to build large audiences from the ground up using sophisticated targeting analytics. For many marketers, it is turning the legacy targeting model of mass media upside down, highlighting the importance of an audience of one, which is then scaled through technology to build custom audiences necessary to execute a specific campaign including real time feedback on creative.

The rapid growth of data, analytics and ad technology including programmatic buying using real-time bidding for impressions is disrupting the traditional media revenue model which is heavily reliant upon advertising. Evolving data-driven ad technology combined with a tsunami of new impressions created through increased time spent with digital media on mobile devices have been responsible for significant share shifts to digital at the expense of traditional media. On its present trajectory, the estimates are for digital ad revenue to surpass $100 billion by 2020 or close to 50 percent of the expected total U.S. advertising market. This is a staggering figure that will serve to both drive and fund the convergence of traditional and new media.

The vast amounts of user data derived from online activities combined with the sophisticated algorithms to help make sense of it are quickly changing the calculus for marketers. Building audiences at scale by aggregating individuals had been more of a marketer's fantasy than a standard operating procedure for developing a media plan. Moreover, the ability to serve dynamic ads that consistently put the right message in front of the right consumer at the right time had also been unthinkable until now. Additionally, the concept of distributed commerce where consumers are exposed to a dynamic ad and then choose to buy the featured product while on an unrelated platform with a simple command has also not been a viable option to date. Modern Media will usher in a new golden age for marketers who will be increasingly focused on consumer touch points that drive business outcomes. The advancements in marketing and commerce will also serve to compel new business models as traditional media companies will be required to innovate with new, bespoke ad products, cutting-edge ad technology and content integrations or cede share of ad spend and consumer engagement.

Media and technology are absolutely converging as the content, distribution and monetization ecosystems for traditional and new media continue to come together. Google and Facebook who together account for more than a quarter of all the ad dollars spent in the U.S., along with digital content distributors including Netflix, Apple, Amazon and Hulu, are collectively becoming the dominant players in the rapidly growing digital distribution ecosystem. They are leveraging data and technology to build distribution businesses capable of owning the customer relationship and serving responsive ads and personalized content to consumers across all connected devices.

Marketers' relationship with media is also changing as they look to the tech companies armed with data to answer the proverbial question about the other half of their ad spend which doesn't work. Moreover, the shift to mobile along with most consumers' near continuous engagement with their mobile devices, gives marketers a plethora of options to serve dynamic and responsive ads to individual users even when they're not consuming media, but rather banking, making dinner reservations, hailing a ride, booking a flight or buying a pair of shoes.

INTERACTIVE CONTENT DELIVERED OVER IP TO PERSONAL SCREENS

The accelerating shift to interactive or IP-based content delivered on demand through mobile devices will continue to disrupt legacy distribution models. Content will increasingly be disaggregated from "bundles" including newspapers, magazines and linear channels, residing in the cloud with an individual address that can be called on demand. The impact will be particularly felt in video as online and offline video converge. Consumers prefer their video content on demand and television networks will respond with OTT offerings that combine their linear channels with large on-demand libraries. Traditional multichannel video programming distributors (MVPDs) and OTT distributors like Apple TV and Roku will continue to innovate the user-interface to make the transition between online and linear television a seamless viewing experience. Digital OTT competitors including Netflix, Hulu, Amazon and YouTube are becoming the next generation of television networks and their subscription-based, on-demand models are giving them increasing leverage in their effort to secure key content assets. The traditional broadcast and cable networks will be compelled to transition their business models and product offerings to remain competitive for viewership and viable for both advertising and subscription revenue.

IP distribution will also become the dominant platform for newspapers as a significant number of daily newspapers will no longer print in the coming decade and with most others scaling back the number of days per week they publish print editions. Newspapers will invariably become much smaller businesses as distribution inexorably moves online and they will likely cede their own digital distribution channels to the incumbent, scaled digital platforms like Facebook, Google and Verizon's AOL and Yahoo as they seek more traffic, advanced ad tech and lower fixed costs.

Exceptions to the disruptive and accelerating shift to IP distribution are satellite and broadcast radio as both have secure distribution channels in the car well into the next decade, in addition to the fact that the average life of a car now exceeds 10 years. Broadcasters and SiriusXM will have the unique advantage over television and newspapers in their ability to continue to derive value from their proprietary distribution channels. Both will need effective mobile distribution strategies to remain relevant for consumers and marketers, but these digital offerings will serve as a necessary complement rather than a substitute as it has become for print journalism.

Select magazine segments including luxury, fashion and interiors will also be more immune from wholesale shift from print media to online. Readers and select advertisers will continue to ascribe value to print media when the content is image-oriented and not time-sensitive. For these select segments, digital distribution will be a necessary complement to a multiplatform branded-experience rather than a substitute for inevitable obsolescence, which again, is the probable case for newspapers and newsweekly magazines.

The rapid shift to mobile IP distribution has been driven by the seminal shift in consumer behavior prompted originally by the launch of Apple's iPhone. To put it in perspective, mobile-based ads were practically nonexistent in 2010, but are widely expected to be the single largest global ad segment by 2020. The last sentence is worth rereading because of the significant impact it will have on evolution of every media business dependent upon advertising. Smartphone penetration is approaching saturation in the U.S. with consumers now spending several hours a day engaged with their mobile devices for communication, information, shopping, entertainment, banking and dozens of other uses to manage their daily lives.

Mobile's impact on society cannot be overstated as it has fundamentally changed consumer behavior associated with these activities for the vast majority of Americans. Ultimately, media reflects the key trends in society and the shift to mobile has been instrumental in both the development of and disruption by the digital media ecosystem including music, video, journalism, gaming and ad tech.

Consumers have become empowered through mobile applications to take greater control of their time, affairs, activities and purchases driven by the inherent and obvious benefits of convenience and efficiency. As mobile apps and their use cases continue to grow, the value of the mobile device, as well as consumer's time spent with it, will both continue to increase. Mobile has truly become an unprecedented behavioral change agent that is both empowering and engaging consumers, particularly in the area of media, communications and commerce.

The constant availability and ease of switching between apps or use cases is shortening attention spans, encouraging multitasking, and altering the way people interact as visual-based messaging apps and images become the preferred method for communication among Millennials and teens. Messaging apps themselves are evolving into multimedia communication platforms that are quickly becoming the next global phenomenon that will impact media content and distribution. These emerging messaging platforms will define the future of global communication with Google, Apple, Amazon, Facebook and others building predictive, voice-based search engines that also catalogue all content inside apps and sites. It's presaging a "post-app" world where virtual assistants driven by machine learning and artificial intelligence "coach" you through your day and anticipate your needs including information and entertainment.

SUBSCRIPTION OFFERINGS WILL BE AN ESSENTIAL REVENUE STREAM

Traditional media companies can no longer count on advertising revenue as a growth driver. As linear mediums, both television and radio have fixed inventory loads and both mediums are experiencing slow but steady audience erosion due to digital fragmentation and the increasing time spent on mobile devices. Fixed inventory and declining audience by itself poses a revenue growth challenge for television and radio, but it is further compounded by an ever-increasing supply of digital inventory availed to the marketplace, which continues to drive the overall cost per impression lower.

Moreover, the traditional pay television ecosystem will continue to contract through a combination of cord cutting and a changing product mix towards skinny bundles in the face of growing OTT competition. Newspapers and magazines face a similar quandary with falling circulation due to lower physical copy sales and compounded by lower CPM's for both legacy and digital impressions.

In order to sustainably grow revenue, media companies will require new product strategies to generate diversified revenue streams away from advertising. Subscription and other fee-based offerings will be a key opportunity for companies to drive incremental revenue by monetizing their audience directly. Consumers have demonstrated a willingness to pay for exclusive content be it video, audio, text or live events. Media companies will need to aggressively look beyond their traditional business models to leverage their content across multiple platforms and also, more importantly, to leverage their promotional platforms in order to monetize their audiences directly through subscription content, live event and select commerce offerings.

Crafting a vision for the future of media in the "modern" era requires an analysis of individual media industry structures against a framework of content, distribution and monetization within the context of anticipated changes in technology, including mobile, cloud computing, IoT and their collective impact on consumer behavior. The media companies of the future will give consumers access to virtually every piece of content ever produced streaming live or on demand on smartphones, watches, tablets, laptops, desktops, televisions, video walls, appliances and automobiles; and content will be sponsored though dynamic and interactive advertising and/or sold directly to consumers as a subscription service. That is the essence of The New Modern Media—a gradual convergence of traditional media's core strengths in entertaining and informing mass audiences with the data rich, IP-based and individually addressable mobile distribution platforms that currently exist at scale across the globe. Publishers, marketers and most importantly, consumers will all benefit from the convenience and personalization of the connected new "modern media," but this kind of change does not come without the attendant disruption to legacy business models and evolving industry structures.

TRANSITION TO A MULTIPLATFORM, DEVICE-AGNOSTIC MODEL

Think of the multiplatform transformation as moving from a linear, medium-centric model to a nonlinear, brand-centric model capable of delivering a highly personalized user experience for both content and advertising. The legacy media industry is structured around mediums including television networks and local affiliates, radio stations, newspapers and magazines. They all cover news, information, sports, entertainment and culture, but do so with very little cross-platform integration.

Serving branded content and ads across multiple platforms or screens, enables media companies and marketers to engage target consumers on their own terms, which is the essence of personalized media. The commercial success of these integrated and personalized offerings will require a multiplatform strategy in order to generate the multiple revenue streams necessary to drive growth including advertising, subscription and commerce.

Media companies that successfully position themselves for the future will be built around leading multiplatform brands targeting audience segments and definable communities of interest both large and small. The "department store" concept that defined the original television networks will slowly evolve as consumers will opt for more specific live and on-demand offerings for sports, news and entertainment; and the economics of competing against the expanding array of subscription-based digital distributors will necessitate greater investment in both content and marketing to remain relevant.

2 | PAST IS PROLOGUE

Marshall McLuhan coined the famous phrase, "The Medium is the Message" in his 1964 book titled "Understand Media: The Extensions of Man." In the book, McLuhan maintained that the "content of any medium is always another medium." Believing that the medium was actually more important than the message itself was quite provocative at the time as McLuhan challenged society to adopt an almost existential perspective on media and its influence on society.

Radio, television and print were all distinctive mediums, which informed and entertained audiences using unique conventions that suited their specific medium. In other words, they could all report on the same story, but tell it effectively in a very different manner with sound, images or text. This is what prompted McLuhan to conclude that the medium, not the story, was the true message. Analog mediums like newspapers, radio, television and magazines each possess rich and distinctive characteristics, which make them uniquely effective vessels (media) for mass communication. They each served their audiences in different ways based upon their use cases and physical characteristics or constraints such as immediacy or lack of images. They each evolved as industries unto themselves because highly specialized skillsets were required to produce compelling content that leveraged the distinct characteristics of the medium itself.

Similarly, the advertising business also became highly specialized with dedicated teams also focusing on creating compelling messages that leveraged the properties of each unique medium. Advertising is just another form of intent or storytelling that is truly effective when it is optimized against both the medium and the intended audience. Thus, the richness and distinctiveness of analog media supported McLuhan's "The Medium is the Message" theory and the best storytellers and content creators used it to their advantage.

Media companies and Madison Avenue were symbiotically built around these siloed structures of broadcast and print with separate divisions for creative and media buying. The original ad agency delineation of broadcast and print was further specialized into radio, television and print as television became of age and expanded with the advent of cable in the early '80s. Television has since grown to a $70 billion ad category that is the largest and most profitable revenue stream for the creative shops. However, digital advertising is more profitable on the buying side due to the add-on products and services for targeting and analytics and the overall lack of transparency in the buying process due primarily to an extremely large number of publishers or sellers of inventory. The share shift to digital and resulting rapid growth of online advertising, which is expected to surpass television in 2017, has compelled the large ad holding companies to invest digital capabilities in the areas of both creative and ad technology in order to keep up with the demands of the Fortune 1000 marketers. Many of the independent digital advertising agencies formed around the turn of the century have since been acquired to give the large ad holding companies the domain expertise needed to compete for higher-margin digital ad market share.

BACK TO THE FUTURE

A quick recounting of key events in the history of media is both interesting and instructive to gain a helpful perspective on the likely trends that will drive its future. By way of background and a bit of fun trivia, the word *media* actually originates from the ancient country Media, part of the Assyrian empire, which was conquered by Persian emperor, Cyrus the Great. It was in Media that the Persians developed the world's first post office to facilitate communication. The term *communication* itself was derived from the Latin root *communicare* employed by The Roman Empire, who like the Persians, also created what might be described as a mail or postal system, in order to centralize control of the empire from Rome. This enabled the Roman citizens to send personal letters throughout the empire and for Rome to gather knowledge about events and people in its many widespread provinces. Thus, in both ancient Persia and Rome, the postal service was the first *media* or form of communication between people other than speech.

Even in its earliest form, "media" was a definitive channel to enable communication and it continued to evolve over time as technological innovation led to the development of the new tools of the day. Beginning in the mid-15th Century, Guttenberg's printing press was an essential piece of technology that led to widespread production of books and newspapers, which in turn became the first form of *mass communication*. Fast forward to the early 1900s when Thomas Edison developed instruments to facilitate electronic communication including the first two-way radio transmission across the Atlantic in 1906. Electronic communication was soon productized and commercialized for the mass market with the introduction of broadcast radio. It began with the first commercial broadcast in 1920 on KDKA in Pittsburgh and within just 20 years, more than 8 of 10 American homes had a radio where families would gather together in living rooms to listen to news, live sports and entertainment programming.

Television followed suit with its introduction to the American living room following the end of World War II. By 1946 there were less than 50,000 televisions in the entire U.S. and over two-thirds of them were in New York, yet there were over 40 million radios in the people's living rooms across the country. As the GI's were returning home, radio was clearly the mass medium that informed and entertained America, but the post-war adoption of television, however, escalated quickly. By 1954, only about half of Americans had a television in their home, but that figure exploded to a whopping 90 percent by 1962, proving to be a harbinger of mobile adoption rates, which would occur more than 50 years later. The broadcast networks defined television for the American public throughout the 1960s and '70s with the Big Three networks directly competing against one another in news, sports and entertainment programming, but it was the launch of CNN in 1980 that ushered in the new era of cable television's focused product offerings which have grown to over 200 channels today.

As the American public learned to integrate their daily lives with modern mass media almost two generations ago, McLuhan's observations were profoundly thought-provoking. Radio, television and print were highly differentiated mediums and each had a special relationship with the audience. Madison Avenue, operating in what was regarded as the "Golden Age of Advertising," understood the promise and power of the medium and focused their creative efforts on exploiting it. "Ad Men" as they were known, came up with some of the most memorable ad campaigns, logos, mascots and slogans—a number of which are still being used some 50 years later. These iconic campaigns were designed to build memorable and likable brands that consumers could trust and develop bonds with. Branding was a highly effective form of marketing used to differentiate similar products within the same categories ranging from cigarettes and detergent to automobiles and television sets. Some of the period's most memorable campaigns included: Folgers' "The best part of waking up is Folgers in your cup," Kellogg's Frosted Flakes' "It's Grrrrrrrrreat!," Kit Kat's "Gimme a break," "Rice-A-Roni—The San Francisco Treat," Bounty's "The Quick Picker Upper," and Alka Seltzer's "Plop-Plop-Fizz-Fizz," all of which are still being used today.

Print and broadcast media were generally structured as silos within agencies, functioning with separate creative teams leading the brand's creative strategy. Similarly, media buying was also organized with separate print and broadcast teams and to a great extent, remains that way today. Organizational structures in both the media and advertising companies formed to reflect the si-loed approach for planning and buying media and served to create a marketplace where industry-specific sellers for TV, radio and print called on industry-specific buyers for TV, radio and print. Moreover, in radio and television, the teams were further segmented by *national spot* where rep firms placed orders directly into local stations and *network* where advertisers buy time indirectly on stations across the country by purchasing inventory from national networks. Networks aggregate the inventory station by station through barter arrangements as consideration for supplying programming and services to local station affiliates.

Today, the medium is no longer the message because we are quickly moving from a medium-centric environment to a content-centric environment with the emergence of the digital distribution ecosystem. As a result, consumers are becoming distribution channel agnostic and even device agnostic as they move seamlessly from screen to screen, often employing multiple screens simultaneously as they consume media content. Content producers and ad creative teams are now challenged to keep pace with the new possibilities for integrated content and ad campaigns designed for—rather than repurposed for—multimedia platforms which concurrently respond to and help change a target audience's new consumption behavior.

Mobile is without question the driving force behind the content-centric shift by putting the content literally into the consumer's hands. The shift began with music, followed by news and games, with online mobile video now assuming the mantle of the fastest growing media segment. Digital and mobile technology are fundamentally transforming the way content is produced, distributed, consumed and monetized with content brands now transcending individual mediums as consumers gain more control over the personalization of their overall media experience.

Advertisers naturally follow audiences and will increasingly look to the treasure trove of consumer data for targeting, messaging and architecting integrated multimedia campaigns, which will consider the totality of impressions to calculate ROI and overall campaign effectiveness. The technology companies including device makers, applications developers and communication networks are currently out in front of both media and advertising companies with respect to capabilities which is spawning legions of disrupters who are racing to fill the many voids. Consequently, the future of media will be defined by the ultimate merging of the new digital-mobile ecosystem with the existing, legacy model. Traditional mediums and branded content distribution businesses will be compelled to transform themselves or risk irrelevance as consumers move on to an integrated, screen agnostic, multiplatform environment.

3 | RADIO, TV & NEWSPAPER ARE NOW AUDIO, VIDEO & TEXT

Historically, media has been an industry that has mostly experienced rational competition, high margins, high barriers to entry and tremendous profits. Newspapers, magazines, radio and television companies all enjoyed a terrific run over the last 50 years. Industries or companies that realize high levels of sustained profitability generally have structural characteristics, which limit competition through intellectual property protections or barriers to entry due to capital requirements or regulatory statutes. For example, you can't purchase a transmitter and antenna and start a radio or television station without navigating the labyrinth of FCC regulations. Conversely, anyone could launch a newspaper in New York or Los Angeles, but the initial capital required to launch a daily newspaper coupled with years of operating losses required to take on an incumbent would make the venture cost prohibitive.

The future of media in the Digital Age is not difficult to imagine. We all have smartphones, which can instantly become television sets, radios, newspapers and magazines. We can watch our favorite shows, listen to our favorite songs, follow our favorite teams or get the weather any time of the day, all from virtually anywhere in the country or the planet for that matter. These liberating and empowering capabilities are the result of digital technology and broadband networks, which are forever changing the way we live.

Enabled by technology, the new digital media ecosystem formed around content, distribution and monetization, has already created significant disruption of the traditional media business beginning with newspapers and music and is now squarely focused on television. Technology is always ahead of commercial application because the innovation of new products and forms has to work its way through legacy beliefs and structures, which takes time. This also represents the advantage of the disrupters who have no turf to protect and the luxury of competing strictly on offense.

Exhibiting characteristics of a classic disrupter, the parallel new digital media ecosystem threatens to subsume the traditional model because it may ultimately be perceived as a superior alternative by both consumers and marketers. More probable, however, is that both digital and traditional media ecosystems will each leverage their inherent strengths leading them to ultimately combine in the coming decade to create the next generation of media and communications.

The inevitable transformation will largely occur over many years and each traditional media business will be impacted differently. The newspaper and record companies should serve as cautionary tales regarding the strategic value of proprietary distribution to the profitability and success of media business models. Traditional media companies will need to harness the power of digital technology to leverage their existing strengths in content and distribution while recognizing the fundamental changes in consumer behavior due to mobile, social and messaging platforms, which are the key drivers of the new digital media ecosystem.

THE SHIFT FROM ANALOG TO DIGITAL

In today's digital world, the analog mediums of radio, television and newspaper have become audio, video and text. By way of definition, analog is a mechanism through which data is represented by continuously variable, physical quantities. A much simpler explanation of analog in the context of media distribution is that analog is a medium that is "spatial" versus the digital medium, which is virtual. For example, a digital clock displays the "data" of time with LED lights in the form of a number whereas an analog clock uses physical "hands" which rotate spatially around the dial to indicate the time.

Conversely, digital is virtual or non-spatial and represents data with discrete values in a binary format (o's and 1's) as opposed to the continuous spectrum of an analog medium. The difference between analog and digital is an important concept to grasp because it is the foundation for the evolution of media. As technology advances, innovation occurs and tools used to create and distribute content become more powerful. As audio, video, text and images all transition from analog to digital formats, the physical boundaries that separated them, as well as the distinctive mediums that were built around them, all begin to converge.

This creates both enormous challenges and opportunities for content creators, distributors and marketers. Long held beliefs and practices must be reimagined because digital content is now consumed on devices designed to bring binary bits to life through video, audio, images and text. Media and advertising companies that have historically been structured in silos are now rethinking both organizational structure and workflow processes to more effectively and efficiently meet the needs of their clients. What was once purposefully separate is now beginning to consolidate around audio, video and display. Television will be the predominant component of video advertising, just as radio will be the predominant component of audio advertising, but they will become increasingly integrated with online offerings featuring interactive components measured in a uniform metric that will most likely be impression-based as the share shift to digital advertising continues.

In the future, consumers won't watch linear television or read the printed newspaper, but rather they will mostly consume on-demand, nonlinear content that will take different forms depending upon the use case and the device or personal screen. It will likely involve multiple screens (unless driving) and feature interaction with various communities of friends and fans, as well as the content creators and presenting sponsors. Advertisers will follow consumers, so the evolving nature of how content is produced and distributed, is making the case for a more integrated approach to marketing across multiple media platforms including social and messaging.

For marketers and content creators, the digital medium is a superior technology to legacy analog mediums because it enables content to be: 1) addressable, 2) nonlinear, and 3) interactive. These three features combine in a very powerful way enabling digital media to create a highly personalized content experience for the consumer. This allows both content creators and marketers endeavoring to engage target consumers with more compelling messaging that is personalized and also potentially interactive. Digital media will eventually surpass conventional analog mediums if they don't evolve their products and strategies just as the mobile phone has largely taken the place of the landline phones at home. Consumers are migrating to more attractive options in digital media driven by the three principal reasons discussed below:

DIGITAL MEDIA IS ADDRESSABLE

Traditional mediums like radio, television, newspaper and magazines all historically delivered their content on a "one-to-many" basis and have done so with a positive ROI for advertisers. The traditional business model worked for both content providers and marketers because consumers have had very limited choices within each medium. More specifically, in the analog world, people can listen to more than 25 different local radio stations and they can choose between 150 or more channels on television, as well as dozens of print options in magazines along with at least one local daily newspaper.

In a "one-to-many" analog world, large and unconnected communities of users formed around popular content assets such as a hit show, a popular morning DJ, a trusted news team or favorite sports columnist. In each case, the content has a following and advertisers can access these audiences using estimates from companies like Nielsen to value the ads. It was the best option for marketers to reach a mass audience to drive awareness and branding for a product or service. The age-old axiom with marketers first coined by famous merchant John Wanamaker in the 19th Century is that half their advertising dollars don't work—they just don't know which half. Mass marketing enables marketers to cost effectively reach large audiences, but the message is broad by design and therefore not as personalized or engaging as it could otherwise be crafted in a digital environment where individual users are addressable and targeting data is plentiful.

This traditional ecosystem functioned quite well in a vacuum, but is now coming under competitive pressure as consumption is fragmenting under increased competition from digital offerings with superior analytics for targeting, engagement and ROI measurement. Think of analog media delivering content as "one-to-many" and digital media as "one-to-one" because consumers are not individually addressable by analog mass media. Digital technology enables the content providers and their advertisers to "address" individual users with their own distinct two-way data stream. A glimpse of the future is here today as users can customize their preferences with any number of sites and apps to create a bespoke offering of content that they find most interesting including news, sports, entertainment, music or even traffic and weather. Digital content is streamed and every stream is unique because it's individually addressed to a user.

Serving addressable content inherently implies that content providers have information about who, what, when and where they serve content which is also of enormous value to marketers seeking to buy and serve smarter ads. The ability to serve addressable content doesn't always mean different content, as in the case of a live sporting event or State of the Union speech, but it makes the consumer more valuable to the marketer because the advertising sold within the standard or non-customized content can be optimized using data against the individual consumer being served. The potential to serve smarter, individually targeted messages is the true value of addressable, digital media content distributed across all connected devices.

Contrast this to a "broadcast" which is "one" signal that can be picked up by "many" users with no return feedback loop. This concept is important to understand because it speaks to the fundamental difference between traditional and digital media. The digital "stream" can be customized for each individual user based upon their explicit demands or based upon information available to content providers such as the sites they visit or even the conversations they have. On the content side, this translates into custom news feeds that match individual users' most particular interests, as well as personalized entertainment feeds such as playlists or videos. It should be noted that not all consumers want custom, on-demand content all the time, but digital media has given the consumer the continuous option. However, as more consumers realize what's available to them, they are sampling alternatives and modifying their media consumption behavior to incorporate these new choices to varying degrees.

Addressability in advertising means that marketers can target specific consumers with tailored messages. In short, it means serving smarter ads to people at more opportune times. Again, the classic marketer's dilemma is understanding which half of their ad spend is wasted. Most tackle the challenge by refining their marketing and media strategies to be more of a rifle-shot as opposed to a shotgun blast. The digital promise of data-driven addressability has been the primary driver of the seminal ad share shift from traditional media to online advertising. The simple premise—and promise—was that smarter impressions would lead to higher ROI's for marketers who invested in digital media. The results, however, are not yet entirely conclusive for various reasons we will analyze in Chapter 15 which examines digital advertising technology. Nevertheless, the addressable characteristics of digital media will continue to be of enormous benefit to marketers as digital content streams are served to individual users via wireline broadband (cable & DSL) or mobile or wireless broadband via LTE or Wi-Fi. The promise and potential to address individual users anytime, anywhere and on any device will be realized over time and lead to deeper changes in the way media companies and marketers engage their audiences.

DIGITAL MEDIA IS NONLINEAR

Consumers got their first taste of a nonlinear alternative to television with TiVo and DVRs. For the first time, they were able to time-shift programs and fast-forward through both content and commercials. Consumers were no longer tied to appointment viewing, but liberated to program their own custom TV experience, albeit with a selection of programs limited by their current pay TV providers. Nevertheless, time-shifting became quite popular as consumers took advantage of this exciting new way to watch television. Gone were the days of rushing home from dinner to watch your favorite prime-time drama. Viewers' relationship with their television set became more proactive as it now served at the pleasure of the viewer rather than the other way around. Consumers learned to control their viewing experience both vertically and horizontally throughout the day and week. For people with time-constrained schedules, the ability to time-shift television viewing was a material improvement to their media consumption experience.

An unintended consequence for marketers was that the timeliness of commercial message delivery was slipping out of their control. If a merchant was promoting a weekend sale and the Thursday show was not viewed until Sunday evening, the message was of little or no value to them. The second and perhaps more significant unintended consequence was the consumer's ability to skip the ads altogether when replaying the broadcast. Moreover, products like Hopper from Dish automatically skip the commercial breaks on playback giving consumers a seamless, ad-free viewing experience. As time shifting became popular, Nielsen ratings, which captured live viewing, began to reflect the shift in behavior with rating declines of live viewing. Media companies appealed to

Nielsen to update their methodology and they responded with C3, which includes any commercial viewed within 3 days of airing. Ratings, however, continued to fall and media companies again appealed to Nielsen to address their methodology by extending the grace period to seven days, which they did with C7.

Advertisers are divided on whether or not to accept C7 and what kind of discount to place on the number of viewers who skip the ads altogether in a nonlinear viewing environment. Early limitations around the amount of content that could be recorded due to storage capacity prevented a wholesale change in viewing habits. Viewers didn't have the ability to record endless programs, creating a library of digital content for viewing at a later date. Time shifting was a small step, but it falls well short of a true nonlinear experience afforded by the on-demand platforms that will ultimately complement or even replace linear channels.

Radio, newspapers and magazines are all linear mediums in their analog form. Consumers are limited to watching, listening and reading whatever the programmers or publishers broadcast or print. In the case of linear electronic media like television and radio, absent time shifting, the consumer has no ability to navigate or interact with the programming, so it becomes what is known as a passive or lean-back experience. In contrast, a nonlinear media experience requires a more active or lean-forward participation by the user to control the experience including choice, sequencing and schedule.

In the digital world, audio, video, text and images are all converted to "bits" or digital data that can be called on demand. This data can be reconstituted, stored and served on a "one-to-one" basis whenever and wherever and on whichever device the consumer demands. Initially, the ability to distribute nonlinear media had the most profound impact on news and information content—both print and broadcast. In a strictly analog environment, the morning newspaper, drive time radio and the nightly news were the primary sources for information on news, weather, sports and traffic. Consuming this information on a daily basis in an exclusively linear format is now completely anathema to the way most people live in today's connected world. We no longer need to watch the weather report on the 11 o'clock news to help plan the next day. The same is true for sports scores or stock market reports. We now have instant access to all of the essential information and consumers have been quick to take advantage of these new digital offerings as evident by the declines in newspaper circulation and television news ratings as the time spent with mobile devices and digital media was ramping up.

Media business models are all feeling the pressure from digital disrupters, but no legacy media business has been more adversely impacted by the shift from analog to digital than daily newspapers. Newspapers have clearly been disrupted by the shift to online news sources as evidenced by their physical circulation, which has declined in 14 of the past 15 years since 2000. As with all media, advertisers inevitably follow audience and because of severe declines in readership of the physical paper, the newspaper industry's revenue has fallen over 60 percent from $50 billion to less than $20 billion today, according to Pew.

These industry numbers include the digital revenue from both advertising and subscriptions, so apples-to-apples on the print product (advertising and sub-scription/newsstand sales) are down even more and continue to decline at double digit rates. Worse yet, they can no longer rely on the high-margin classified reve-nue to support the business because due to online competitors like Craigslist and eBay, newspaper classified revenue has been hit even harder. Across the country, newspapers have shed tens of thousands of jobs as local papers increasingly look to national and regional wire services to fill the content void as fewer journalists are left in the newsroom to cover important local and regional beats.

The conundrum for local newspapers is that technology now facilitates a 24-hour news cycle, but news organizations are strapped due to the precipitous decline in ad revenues and are often not able to afford the resources necessary to produce the quality content their readers demand. The void in coverage has been filled by bloggers, citizen journalists and digital news sites with widely varying levels of journalistic integrity. With little or no barriers to entry, there are now well over a million bloggers who are actively publishing content on everything imaginable and aggregators like Alltop, Google Reader and Tumblr and many others are making it easier to discover and access this content. Consumers now have exponentially more choice and are therefore dramatically less reliant on the traditional print media that has essentially controlled journalism for close to a century.

DIGITAL MEDIA IS INTERACTIVE

Interactivity is one of the most exciting aspects of digital media because it creates the potential for a deeper, two-way engagement with the consumer. In a highly fragmented content environment with entry barriers falling, engagement is becoming increasingly more important for both media companies and marketers. Interactivity is a form of virtual dialogue where consumers can provide real-time feedback to help improve their viewing, listening or reading experience. In turn, content providers can fine-tune their products to better serve their customers on an individual basis. This heightened level of interaction helps build a stronger relationship with the consumer, which leads to higher and more sustained levels of usage. For example, music streaming services like Pandora or Spotify can get instant feedback from listeners on song preferences to adjust playlists by capturing data that also helps identify trending content that can be introduced to other users to improve their music discovery experience. Likewise, digital news services can fine-tune content to match a reader's interest in politics, business, sports, crime, etc. The same is true for digital video services like YouTube or Facebook which can suggest individual videos or multi-channel networks based upon a user's viewing history and interests while identifying content producers who are trending to help improve the viewing experience.

Advertisers reap obvious and immediate benefits from interactive marketing messages. In an online environment, marketers can appeal to consumers to take immediate action including watch a video, visit a site, order a product or request more information and affiliate with the brand through social media. For this reason, interactive engagement is perhaps even more important to marketers who, through the very nature of advertising, are basically interrupting content to communicate with target consumers.

A message perceived as an intrusion can leave a negative impression on a brand, whereas a message that connects on a personal level is generally accretive to the brand. The key takeaway is that for both content producers and marketers, the potential for heightened levels of engagement are tremendous, but the path to success is not clear and much experimentation will be required, though core marketing and branding fundamentals will apply. Great advertising in the form compelling storytelling, however, is rarely perceived as intrusive in any format.

Many years ago, I traveled to Detroit to hear W.B. Doner give a speech. Doner was one of the great "ad men" of his generation and responsible for the famous Timex slogan, "It takes a licking and keeps on ticking." He gave a wonderful speech about his storied experiences in the ad business and in his closing remarks, he said that after all his years in the advertising business, he developed two immutable axioms: First, "you gotta stop 'em to sell 'em." Even in a prior generation, there was sufficient ad clutter that Doner recognized that he couldn't effectively communicate a message to an audience if he didn't first grab their attention. In today's short attention span society where people multitask while consuming media, the notion of capturing a prospect's attention in order to "sell 'em" is more important than ever.

Doner's second axiom was: "People buy from people they like." This is an immutable law for both marketing and sales—and most of life for that matter. Individual addressability, custom tailored messaging across multiple platforms and interactive communication are all effective tools for marketers to engage with target consumers on a deeper level to build stronger relationships, more efficiently and expeditiously. Today's marketers strive to convert consumers into fans of brands to build a personal connection that they hope to spread through their fan's social graphs.

Doner and his peers were practicing their craft in a strictly analog world through traditional media's "one-to-many" formats. Digital media's one-to-one interactivity provides a much more robust tool kit for marketers to both "stop 'em" with a compelling and relevant message and to create an affinity for a brand through consistent messaging enhanced with interactivity through social media and other platforms to drive deeper engagement.

Moreover, the ability to interact with consumers on an individual basis gives marketers the ability to expand the message to other platforms such as company websites and apps, as well as social platforms like Facebook, Instagram, Snapchat and Twitter. It's early in the lifecycle of interactive content for both programmers and marketers, but the promise is great to help marketers both "stop 'em" and make friends with their target consumers.

4 | APPLE:
THE FIRST MODERN PLATFORM

Ironically, Apple is not widely thought of as a media company, but it has had a profound impact on the way people create and distribute digital media content throughout the world. The genius of Apple lies in the elegance and simplicity of both its form and functionality. They have created an inviting and intuitive user experience integrating hardware, software and services to fundamentally change the way we communicate, consume media, transact and generally run our lives. Long before the iPhone and iPad entered our lexicon, Apple was a niche computer company targeting the consumer, education and publishing markets. Its products were well regarded, but the relatively closed-architecture it employed relegated it to a small, but fiercely loyal consumer segment. The Apple DNA of creating user ecosystems built around hardware, software and services that took root with the Macintosh is evident today in their music, television, publishing and nascent payments ecosystems with the music business becoming Apple's first major success in expanding beyond a niche computer company into mass market consumer electronics and digital commerce.

ITUNES — BUILDING AN ECOSYSTEM

Prior to Apple's entry in digital music in 2001, digital audio was in a nascent form. Applications like SoundJam and others enabled users to rip audio files from CDs, download them to a PC and burn them back to a CD. Consumers had migrated from analog cassette tapes to digital format CDs and were being conditioned to expect superior sound quality from the new digital music technology. Consumers built their music collections around CDs and automakers followed suit, incorporating CD players into their dashboard entertainment systems while home entertainment systems weren't complete without a multi-disk CD player. The size of the CD, compared to a cassette tape, didn't lend itself to a portable version however, which created an opening for Apple to innovate the category, making the cumbersome size of the portable CD players a perceived vulnerability that made the introduction of the iPod that much more appealing.

In addition to ripping and burning CDs, audio file transfers became possible beginning in 1997 through AOL Messenger and other services. Digital music file sharing became mainstream, however, with the launch of Napster in 1999. The controversial, free file-sharing service became a cult sensation, growing quickly to well over 20 million users. Its mission was piracy, pure and simple. Someone would purchase a CD, rip it and upload it to Napster, then anyone could download the file and burn it to a CD for free. The service was, not surprisingly, sued by A&M Records in early 2001 and forced to shut down later that year. Steve Jobs and his team were obviously following these developments and it led them to purchase SoundJam MP which was a popular application used to rip CDs on to Apple's Macintosh computer. SoundJam's technology later became the basis for iTunes, which was launched in 2001.

Apple's foray into digital media through the iPod was the first phase of an architected end-to-end solution for digital audio. The next important component in the ecosystem was the introduction of the iTunes Store, which created an easy way for iPod owners to legally download their favorite music, as well as giving them the ability to carry their entire record collection (or the record store for that matter) in their pocket or purse. For many consumers who primarily used CDs, it was their first exposure to the process of the digital downloading of music. Consumers were quickly being conditioned to the realization that media could exist in a digital form as opposed to the physical medium that people were accustomed to purchasing and playing.

The first iPod was introduced in 2001 and could hold up to 1000 songs that could be downloaded from your PC. By the end of 2002, Apple had sold 600,000 iPods, but it wasn't until they launched the iTunes Store in 2003 that sales began to take off. Within two years, Apple had sold 42 million iPods and just two years later in 2007, they had sold 142 million iPods and over 3 billion songs in the iTunes Store. These are staggering numbers for a new product launch, which fundamentally changed the way people bought and consumed to music in just a few short years. By 2010, Apple had sold 275 million iPods and 10 billion songs.

Looking upstream in the value chain, at the time of the iPod launch, the music companies were healthy and profitable with global sales approaching $30 billion in 2000. Things were about to change for labels, however, as the ability to rip and burn CDs along with illegal file sharing supported by Napster and others was threatening to cannibalize sales as the youth generation who are typically heavy music consumers, were actively sharing music files and beginning to buy less product. Feeling the pinch of piracy and after much consternation, the labels collectively agreed to sell their music digitally through Apple's new online retail channel named the iTunes Store. In true Apple form, it was brilliantly designed to provide an integrated and seamless user experience with Apple's iPod and consumers quickly embraced it making the iTunes store an overnight success.

The unintended consequence of this success, however, was a precipitous drop in music sales from 2000 to 2010. So while Apple was selling over $10 billion of music at 99 cents a song, the music industry's revenue was in free fall due to a combination of continued piracy and the consumer's new preference for singles over albums. Apple had successfully created an ecosystem for music that simultaneously displaced the physical retail channel for music while disaggregating the bundle of songs known as the album—the latter was a harbinger for digital distribution's impact on most every aspect of the media business.

By 2008, Apple had displaced WalMart to become the world's largest music retailer up from 10th place two years earlier when iconic Tower Records closed the doors on 89 of its stores. Apple was doing to standalone music retailers what Amazon had done to standalone book retailers. Cost, choice and convenience drove consumers to a new digital distribution channel, which offered a superior user experience driven also by online connectivity. For the traditional retailers, the resulting drop in physical sales left them unable to meet the high fixed operating costs of brick-and-mortar retail storefronts. This painful scenario will be replayed many times in the future across a number of retail channels and service businesses as consumers become more conditioned to buying goods and services online.

The positive effect of the iTunes ecosystem was greater overall consumption of music. As iPod sales approached one for every person in the country, the access to on-demand music was greater than ever before. Access, portability, ease of use and affordability were the keys to widespread adoption and the "closed" iTunes ecosystem prevented any serious competitive threat from gaining traction. It was brilliantly architected and executed and resulted in an enormous value transfer from labels and music retailers to Apple's shareholders as iTunes grew to account for up to 50 percent of music sales worldwide. It's extremely rare for one company to enter a large global market like recorded music, and turn it upside down, virtually gutting the industry's profitability without competing directly against the label's IP—their artists. In other words, Apple didn't enter the space with their own slate of artists, but rather they convinced the record companies to cede the distribution channel to them while also convincing the labels to disaggregate their highly profitable "bundle" and sell their songs individually for 99 cents each.

The parallel is striking between the recorded music bundle (the album) and the pay television bundle and increasingly with the newspaper bundle being disaggregated by Facebook Instant Articles and others. The music industry sought to address the piracy problem by allowing Apple to effectively gain control of the distribution channel and disaggregate their highly profitable bundle. In retrospect, they would have been better served to allow only limited singles just as they had in the album-age with the physical medium and preserved the bundle (album) while addressing piracy aggressively both in the courts, as well as the court of public opinion through an aggressive artist-led campaign in partnership with broadcast radio.

iTUNES PAVED THE WAY FOR STREAMING VIDEO

Within two years of launching the iTunes store for music, Apple was also selling digital downloads of movies and television shows through the iTunes Store. By 2006, Apple had sold 50 million television episodes and 1.3 million feature-length films. The iTunes ecosystem had successfully conditioned consumers that all media could be downloaded via a digital format and consumed on demand through a range of devices including portable iPods, as well as laptops and desktop computers. The concept of physical media like CDs and DVDs was becoming obsolete, laying the groundwork for the Amazon Kindle, which was launched in 2007. The Kindle eReader and Kindle Store were essentially a replica of the iTunes ecosystem for books. Books were converted to digital files and downloaded on a device for on-demand access similar to music on an iPod. Unlike music, however, e-books account for only about 20 percent of the books sold in the U.S. and appears to be holding steady at that number. Americans still want to read physical books, but they are buying the majority of them through an online retailer.

It was also in 2007 that Netflix introduced digital streaming of movies, but did so as an extension of their highly successful subscription model. They were capitalizing on consumer demand for digital media streaming for on-demand consumption. Because of Apple's innovation, by 2007, music, books, movies and television shows were all being distributed digitally through downloads. Fast forwarding to today, the digital video marketplace is extremely competitive with the studios largely profitable and growing with the increase consumption of video content. Contrast this to the music industry, which permitted Apple to create a comparatively closed ecosystem eliminating competition while disaggregating the album as the industry's greatest source of profits. The studios had the benefit of studying the structural changes to the record industry and the negative impact they had on sales and profits. As a result, Apple will likely emerge as a strong competitor in video, but it's highly unlikely that they will achieve the market power in television and motion picture distribution that they have achieved in music unless they shift their strategy and enter the content business.

A seminal year for media and technology, 2007 saw Netflix launch a streaming video service while Amazon's Kindle eReader, the Kindle was introduced to stream text and images found in printed books to portable devices. The success of Netflix's streaming video offering spawned the over-the-top (OTT) on-demand video market which is driving the current digital disruption of television. Likewise, the Kindle served as the entry point into digital media for the world's largest online retailer. They would leverage the experience to transition the offering into today's Amazon Prime subscription service including digital books, music, television, film and games on demand. It's instructive to understand the evolution of the leading digital companies as they enter markets, launch products and expand their scope. Netflix, Amazon and Apple are three examples of companies that have effected enormous value transfers from existing media content and distribution businesses to their respective balance sheets by leveraging technology and the network effect to provide consumers with superior alternatives.

THE iPHONE-INSPIRED MOBILE REVOLUTION

The other newsworthy product introduction of 2007 also ushered in the era of mobile computing, which became the next quantum leap for digital media. The launch of the iPhone in 2007 followed by the introduction of the iPhone 3G and the launch of the App Store in 2008, which together created the unprecedented consumer adoption rates of the smartphone and their behavioral shift to mobile. This burgeoning new Apple ecosystem was built on a revolutionary new user experience, which was at once, intuitive and progressive, and led to rapid adoption and imitation by competitors.

Consumer's adoption of the smartphone technology was fueled by the rapidly growing app ecosystem, which transformed the mobile device into a powerful, pocket-sized PC with thousands of new use cases for consumers and businesses. This began a virtuous circle of increasing consumer demand for mobile devices, exploding app development and robust wireless network upgrades to support the exponential increase in network traffic and data consumption.

This phenomenon helped to transform Apple from a niche computer maker into the world's most valuable company by 2015 with an enterprise value approaching $700 billion. Today, the iPhone accounts for almost two-thirds of Apple's revenue and an even greater share of their profits. Apple's rise has been remarkable, and has been driven almost entirely by the iPhone, which now captures more than 90 percent of the profits of the cell phone industry. Interestingly, though iPhones only account for approximately 20 percent of unit sales, at an average price of $650 per phone versus under $200 for the average Android model, Apple has effectively taken control of an industry that was completely dominated by Nokia and Blackberry at the time Apple entered the market in 2007. Best in-class device design combined with best in-class user experience and thousands of compelling new use cases through apps made it an easy trade for consumers.

Apple employed an iPod-like strategy to drive the success of the iPhone using the App Store to drive iPhone sales much the same way as the iTunes Store drove iPod sales. An expansive array of content and services delivered seamlessly in a fully-integrated ecosystem that created a best-in-class consumer experience. As developers flocked to the platform, the use cases for both the consumer and enterprise increased exponentially driving yet more iPhone sales. The "stickiness" of the integrated ecosystem combined with the user experience and fashionable image of the brand all worked in concert to sustain a premium pricing strategy in the face of a rapidly commoditizing industry. The strategy and execution of Apple's launch of the iPod, followed by the launch of the iPhone and App Store have been nothing short of brilliant, creating hundreds of billions of dollars of value for Apple shareholders. Society has benefited as well with the transformation of the cell phone into a multimedia, portable PC with unlimited use cases that unarguably have had a role in improving consumers' quality of life.

Unlike the iPod and the iTunes Store, the iPhone's launch led to brutal competition in the smartphone market. After several years of competition between hundreds of brands running multiple operating systems including iOS, Android, Symbian, Windows, BlackBerry, Bada and Palm, the industry has consolidated dramatically around just two —Android and iOS.

Moreover, device makers Apple and Samsung (which is powered by Android) account for almost 110 percent of the industry's profits which means the rest of the competing brands, of which there are hundreds, are collectively losing money. The Android operating system is now shipped on more than 80 percent of the phones sold worldwide making it, along with iOS, the top priority for developers and an insurmountable competitive disadvantage for all other competitive entrants as evidenced by Microsoft's retreat from its mobile ambitions through the purchase of Nokia and Windows Mobile OS.

Mobile operating systems are an important example of the network effect where the most popular operating systems become the most valuable platforms to developers, which in turn make the devices running those operating systems most valuable to consumers. It's virtuous circle that has reduced the global market for mobile operating systems to a virtual duopoly.

As mobile devices continue to become more indistinguishable in form and features, the selection of apps and integration with other consumer devices like home entertainment systems, auto dashboards, home infrastructure controls and wearables will shape the user experience and drive perceived value while increasing switching costs. The number of competitors driving a fierce battle for profits should portend frequent and substantial innovation and cost reduction for years to come. Streaming video is an excellent example of the virtuous circle of innovation. Phones are equipped with 1080p or 4k video cameras and software that enable them to capture full motion video. App developers like Facebook, Snapchat and Twitter leverage the mobile phone's capabilities to capture video, offering a distribution platform to build a network of users. Supporting handset makers and app developers are the wireless carriers who are also in a highly competitive battle to acquire and retain customers and consequently, they are making major investments to upgrade their networks to handle the increased demand for data hungry video streaming.

ANOTHER PRODUCT, ANOTHER NEW CATEGORY

After publicly killing the Newton in 1998, Steve Jobs remained steadfastly against a tablet launch until after the iPhone became a runaway hit and ironically, Apple designer, Jonathan Ives had actually worked on a tablet prior to designing the iPhone. The iPhone's touchscreen interface was becoming extremely popular with consumers and along with the expansive App Store, they would combine to serve a tablet product well. The iPad was launched in 2010 as essentially a large version of the iPhone, with a similar display capable of running the iPhone apps. Apple also introduced iBooks as custom media for the iPads and to enable the device to compete directly with the Kindle. The digital book reader was yet another example of the new device's relevant use cases that helped define a new category of a portable computing device running on a mobile operating system.

The iPad also found its place in the enterprise market giving Apple a rapidly growing toehold in a space that had not previously been their province. iPads were used for data displays, electronic controls and multimedia presentation tools for infield personnel to name just a few. Thousands of apps created innovative new use cases in the enterprise and SMB markets which helped cement the iPad's status as another Apple product launch which not only defined a new category, but also laid the predicate for mobile media including online video.

The iPad ramped quickly reaching a peak of 78 million units sold in 2014 before declining in 2015 due to the cannibalization by the larger iPhone 6 Plus. Prior to the launch of larger screen smartphones, iPads were the preferred device for watching videos, television shows and movies, as well as browsing and posting on social media. It was the ability to sit on the couch while watching television and chat with friends on social media that enabled a unique two-screen viewing experience. People would watch programming or play games in a virtual community sharing real-time comments about the content. Multiscreen experiences are routine for Millennials, as well as others who are keenly interested in what people are saying in real time about pop culture, news, entertainment and sports content.

The iPad has also had a lasting impact on people's willingness to consume video content including television and motion pictures on a smaller screen to create a more personalized viewing experience. It represents the first personal television set that is easily programmed through apps and the iTunes Store to create a true on-demand viewing experience with a mobile device. The iPad has changed the way people consume video content, conditioning people that the experience of a mobile device and the convenience of a mobile operating system is a wonderful way to engage with content on a more intimate basis. It helped to create the use cases for on-demand video, multi-screen engagement and a more personalized viewing experience that collectively are driving the evolution of modern media.

WHY APPLE TV WON'T REDEFINE TELEVISION

Apple TV will also play an important role in shaping the consumer experience for television and video consumption, but it's unlikely they will impact the economics of the industry as they have in music and smartphones for several reasons.

In music, Apple was able to capture the market because they were essentially the first to market with an elegant, end-to-end digital solution. They architected an ecosystem that thwarted competition, but needed a willing accomplice in the record labels to execute their plan. The labels were fighting a serious battle with peer-to-peer file sharing services like Napster that were enabling rampant piracy. Consequently, an entire generation of music consumers was being conditioned to believe it was their right to download free, on-demand music. This in turn, drove the labels to Apple's fully baked solution as an organized way of combating piracy, but the disaggregation of the bundle (album) put extreme downward pressure on revenue and profits. Today, the music industry's revenue is split roughly 50/50 between physical and digital product and total revenues have stabilized at half their peak volume. Unlike their original greenfield opportunity to dominate music, Apple doesn't have the first mover advantage in television and is entering a market where their playbook has been widely studied and adopted by competitors like Netflix, Comcast, Sony, HBO, Hulu, Amazon, Google/YouTube and Samsung.

Also unlike the opportunity with music or phones, the television set market is mature, extremely competitive and marginally profitable with the device (TV set) replacement cycle of over five years, more than twice that of smartphones. Apple's entry point with hardware is therefore with the set-top box and controller rather than the set itself, as well as through an operating system that drives the user experience. As the physical screen becomes more commoditized, the controller and operating system become the differentiating features that shape the user experience. With a set-top box and touchscreen or voice activated remote control, Apple can effectively bring the Apple experience for interactive media including streaming video, online games and thousands of new apps developed specifically for an interactive television screen experience which transcend traditional television content. It's more of aftermarket integration rather than a total ecosystem approach with the goal of creating a dynamic new television operating system delivered OTT. The App Store will be a key competitive advantage for Apple as app-developers flock to the new platform. As with smartphones, look for Android to factor aggressively into the competitive offerings as the television's operating system, also with the strong support of the developer community and television set manufacturers.

The myriad of new apps will create an entirely different and incremental dimension of entertainment for the television set resulting in exciting new use cases for both consumers and commercial enterprises. The key to mass adoption will be the blending of traditional, linear content including movies and shows with on-demand video, games and apps designed for the device with an intuitive user experience that seamlessly transitions from one to the other. Similar to the iPhone user experience including the App Store, which was widely matched by Android, Apple will likely innovate the television or large-screen experience with fast followers from present pay television and smartphone ecosystems. Google is aggressively developing a competitive ecosystem integrating the world's most popular mobile operating system with the world's most trafficked digital video distribution site, YouTube, along with the Google Play Store selling all forms of media content. YouTube now represents a material share of Google's (Alphabet) revenue making Google well-positioned to compete for the ad and subscription services side with a device-agnostic mobile ecosystem that continues to solidify its market position through the network effect.

Preserving the current pay TV bundle is clearly in the best interest of the incumbents and effectively relegates Apple to a complementary service rather than a true OTT substitute for cable and satellite MVPDs. Moreover, the programmers already have a plethora of options through both traditional distributors and emerging OTT competitors. They can wholesale their content to distributors, as well as retain their retail options by going direct to consumer with both linear channels as well on-demand options including multimedia offerings similar to the Disney Life product bundle. Comcast has also aggressively innovated the user experience with their Xfinity product and will rightfully view Apple TV with their complement of linear and on-demand content as a direct competitive threat.

The real profitability in video distribution will lie in controlling the customer relationship with respect to content and services. Abdicating this means becoming a dumb pipe and being relegated to selling commoditized broadband which will be under pricing pressure from wireless carriers, wireline and potentially over-builders or even utilities. This has been the plight of heavily regulated wireless carriers (AT&T, Verizon, T-Mobile and Sprint) who have invested heavily in their wireless broadband networks while device makers like Apple and Samsung and online service providers like Facebook, Google, Netflix and Amazon have created hundreds of billions of dollars of value on their backs. This occurred as network operators face cutthroat pricing competition amongst their peers to compete aggressively for each other's customers in a mature market.

The relative success of Apple's late entry into the TV market will depend upon its ability to create an alternative user experience in both form and function just as they were successful in doing with music and mobile phones. They will need the cooperation of content owners, but the model for this is already firmly established. Securing content relationships, however, should be viewed more as table stakes than a product-defining element. The threat of cord-cutting is not the parallel event that the music industry faced with the threat of piracy when they collectively cut their deals with Apple for digital distribution through iTunes. Content owners have a myriad of different digital distributors who want their product. Moreover, through windowing, they can license the same content to multiple distributors for airing at different times to maximize yield. This will likely cause Apple to rethink their video strategy and ultimately acquire a large content company as the Modern Media ecosystem continues to take shape.

Media companies will remain steadfastly unwilling to offer discount rates for their content for an Apple TV consumer offering because they are also well aware of the economic impact from the disaggregation of the content bundle in music (single song in lieu of album). Content owners will be unlikely to make the same mistake by allowing Apple or any other OTT distributor to cherry pick their highest demand content and package it into a more efficient consumer offering as an alternative to the current pay television bundle. Dish's Sling TV and other slimmer packages simply exclude networks or entire network groups. Content owners also have MFNs or most favored nation clauses in their agreements with traditional video distributors that effectively prevent content owners from cutting better deals for new entrants. As such, it will be virtually impossible for Apple or any other OTT distributor to create a demonstrably better consumer offering based upon price alone.

Creating a unique offering with mass market appeal will require giving consumers a refreshingly new use case for all of the consumer's screens ranging from the 50-inch screen in their family room to their PCs, tablets, smartphones and wearables. There is an opportunity to create a connected experience across all screens while making it easier than ever before to program a more traditional television experience including linear, on-demand and user-generated video content both in-home and in a mobile environment. The market is enormous and represents one of the last frontiers in digital media. Consumers will continue to be the beneficiaries with increased choice and convenience at a lower cost.

Similar to the television market, Apple's participation in the intensively competitive and mature global auto market will depend upon their ability to infiltrate the dash with an iPhone-like user interface for entertainment, maps, communication and other services including commerce. Automakers, like MVPDs, are highly protective of their customer relationships and will not willingly cede them to Apple or any other third-party technology company. The entry point for Apple, Google or Microsoft could be a product integration with individual manufacturers as carmakers look to the car's entertainment and operating systems to provide a competitive advantage. The other approach is more indirect leading to a takeover of the dash through a smartphone integration and would obviously be limited to Apple and Google because of the dominate shares of their mobile operating systems. Also, the integration would only be as deep as permitted by the automaker and many would likely want an operating system-agnostic approach so as not to disenfranchise any potential car buyer. Automakers have also learned from the music industry to protect their data and customer relationships. Virtually every car today has an iPod/iPhone direct connect or Bluetooth integration, but that hasn't enabled an Apple takeover of the auto dashboard.

Following the law of large numbers, Apple needs to continue to sell iPhones and innovate new services in order to grow their revenue and profits. Apple's terrific innovations to the user experience are designed to broaden the base of Apple customers and continue to increase switching costs due to convenience, utility, image and perceived value. The auto market will be interesting to watch, but success will depend upon their ability to create an intuitive user experience, which is consistent with their mobile and in-home strategies. Automakers plan their product design and supply chain years in advance, so expect the car to be a longer-term project than television or payments.

APPLE PAY WILL PAYOFF

Payments are also an enormous market, which could give Apple the ability to expand their customer base both in the consumer and enterprise markets. Their initial foray into payments was Apple Pay, which is a payment disbursement app that replaces the need to pull out a credit card. Apple Pay links directly to your credit card company and aside from the reader, the rest of the process is unchanged for the merchant.

It's not dissimilar to downloading a boarding pass on your smartphone in lieu of the paper ticket. Millennials are early adopters and it will likely catch on over time. The catalyst for adoption however is the end-to-end payments solution that multiple tech companies are racing to create. Apple Pay will evolve from a one-way payment disbursements app to a two-way app that receives as well as disburses payments.

The goal for online payments systems is to take over the wallet for the consumer, amass tremendous amounts of purchase data and use it to create a more personalized commerce experience for consumers—not dissimilar to the evolving content and ad experience of modern media. The strategy is to eliminate the need for traditional credit cards for the consumer and to replace the payment services function for the merchant. Successfully creating a direct relationship between the consumer and vendor, the vendor and the bank, and of course, the bank and the consumer, would result in a payments ecosystem that would benefit greatly from the network effect.

Also included in this new service are peer-to-peer transfers. People will be able to transfer money to one another without the need for a check, money order or wire transfer. Think of these services currently as distribution channels for capital that will increasingly be ripe for disintermediation by a mobile payments system. Consumers will welcome the convenience and cost savings as the middlemen—payment processors and even credit card companies—are ultimately marginalized. Apple's key competitive advantage in payments could end up being cost if it chooses to offer the service as a free service to encourage merchants to purchase their devices. Free is tough to compete with as the non-iOS competitors have witnessed with the growth of Android.

Mobile payments are largely an untapped global market that Apple looks to enter with a Trojan Horse strategy of merchant services at little or no cost to create a network effect around payment services leading to a large and new market segment for device sales. Apple's payments strategy is noteworthy for media companies because Apple has demonstrated extreme adroitness in leveraging users from one product or service ecosystem into another. Media, communications, commerce and now financial services are each affected by Apple's products and services. It's important to note that the larger Apple's user base becomes, the more of a competitor they will become to any media business that distributes content.

Apple's success in creating the first "modern platform" has served as a powerful catalyst in the digital transformation of media. Through iTunes,

Apple effectively introduced the mass consumer market to digital downloads, and next to the streaming of audio, video and images. They successfully created a proprietary ecosystem for music that changed the industry structure and forever altered the economics of the music industry. Apple then leveraged this success to transform the mobile phone industry into a mobile communication revolution. Building another ecosystem with devices, an operating system and apps, Apple unleashed the power of mobile networks to connect the world and fundamentally change the way we live. Their continued success in television, payments and even transportation will be, in part, decided by their competitors who have learned from Apple's playbook and developed their competitive strategies accordingly.

Apple has demonstrated the power of a simple and intuitive user interface seamlessly integrated with a trove of content and applications to create an exemplary user experience to drive leading market share at the industry's highest price points. The lesson for content owners is to avoid ceding leverage to a potential ecosystem play by owning the customer relationship including the end-user data. Content owners should be agnostic as to the device and operating system through which their content is consumed, but they are ill advised to permit a digital distributor to disaggregate their proprietary content bundle for the promise of increased traffic and near-term revenue gains.

Distributors including digital music services, pay television (MVPDs), OTT offerings and gaming consoles like Sony PlayStation are in direct competition with Apple's ambitions to control and redefine the television experience on both large screens and mobile devices. The key to preserving their incumbent status and competing successfully against Apple is continued and rapid innovation of their user experience. The perceived switching costs for most consumers give the existing distributors a competitive buffer, but they must remain vigilant in their quest to innovate their product in order to protect their market position and retain their user base. Consumers tend to like what they know more than they know what they like, so incumbency, like inertia, is a powerful force and distributors need to use it to their advantage through constant innovation to create an intuitive, integrated user experience.

A good example of this is Pandora. Though their business model may be challenged due to the high variable cost of royalties, the intuitive user interface and elegant simplicity made it an instant hit with consumers. In a highly competitive space, they now claim over 80 million monthly active users for a service that streams custom playlists for an interactive experience that is described as "lean back" as opposed to the on-demand services where you are selecting each song as if you owned the content. Pandora has risen above the competition because of its ease of use more so than its feature set. It has consistently resisted the temptation to over-engineer its product and has maintained a large and loyal user base.

Steve Jobs said that "simple can be harder than complex" and to compete successfully against Apple, companies need to focus on the simplicity and intuitiveness of their user experience. Media companies must also think of television as simply another screen and strive for a connected and continuous experience as consumers move from one device to another and often employ multiple devices simultaneously. Competitive offerings to the linear pay TV bundle will compete on the three dimensions of content, price and user experience.

5 | MOBILE CHANGED THE WORLD

Few products have fundamentally impacted the world as much as the smartphone led by the iPhone's introduction in 2007 and followed by the first version of Android which was launched later that year. Today there are over 200 million smartphone users in the U.S. and over 2 billion worldwide. Android and Apple have created a virtual duopoly as their mobile operating systems power virtually all of the world's smartphones. In just a few short years, smartphones have become the second most time consuming activity behind watching television. According to eMarketer, Americans now spend more than 3 hours per day on their smartphones texting, talking, watching, listening, reading, sharing, banking and shopping. It's become such an indispensable tool that it's frankly hard to imagine what it was like to live in the proverbial stone ages before the launch of the iPhone.

I can remember starting out in my career in the mid-1980s and routinely using pay phones in airports, train stations, hotels and gas stations. If you were lost, you pulled over and asked for directions, and if you wanted a phone number, you called 411 to reach a live operator. It wasn't that long ago that the speed of business and progress of society was gated by limitations of communication technology. Mobile phones became popular in the 1990s as they evolved from the often-parodied "brick" phone to smaller devices like the iconic Motorola

TAC flip-phone. The cell phone adoption rates grew quickly as the devices and monthly plans became more affordable enabling them to reach critical mass in 1994 when approximately two-thirds of Americans had mobile phones. It was the fastest mass-adopted device in history according to Pew, only to be bested in 20 years by the even faster rate of adoption for smartphones.

The cellphone, now known as a smartphone, is really a globally connected supercomputer that fits in your pocket or purse. The device and its widespread consumer adoption has had a profound impact on society because it has revolutionized the way we communicate, the way we work, the way we shop, the way we socialize, the way we consume media and the way we entertain ourselves. It has brought highly-sophisticated, digital technology to the masses for use in everyday life through thousands of applications or "apps," which enable users to harness the computing power and connectivity of the smartphone.

By the end of 2009, voice traffic was superseded by data traffic on mobile phones and today, voice represents a very small percentage of monthly data consumed over wireless networks. Messaging has become the predominant way people communicate because it's instant and more convenient. The art of conversation and the practice of writing are slowly fading as people gravitate towards a less rich and terser, form of shorthand communication. Pictures and images such as emojis are increasingly serving as suitable substitutes for composing written text. The extreme example that most everyone has witnessed at least once is a group of people (or a family) sitting at a table staring at their phones as they text one another to communicate. Texting is different from email because it's short form, fluid, informal, idiom-based, ephemeral, and now multimedia with voice, image and video messaging options. The ubiquitous messaging apps are rapidly evolving to become multimedia communication platforms with their DNA rooted in the short-form text. Moreover, speech recognition virtual assistants like Amazon's Echo, Apple's Siri, Microsoft's Cortana, Hound and others will gradually move users away from day-to-day interaction with service providers. What is essentially a consumer convenience enabled by technology may have longer term consequences for the way society communicates and interacts as natural language processing continues to evolve.

Mobile has also fundamentally changed the way people work. They are no longer tethered to desks or workstations and are able to access documents or information from virtually anywhere enabling them to be in constant communication with coworkers and clients. As a result, it's changing the concept of an "office" as a fixed base of operations because of the flexibility afforded by smartphones and tablets. Office space today is more open and communal and work schedules are more flexible to improve productivity. Mobile has also spurred demand for cloud computing, which seamlessly connects users with one another as well as with content, data, information or virtually anything with an IP address, which is enabling the rapidly growing Internet of Things (IoT).

Mobile has made every day activities like booking travel arrangements, making dinner reservations, hailing a ride or getting directions as simple as opening an app or engaging a virtual assistant. Shopping has also been forever changed with the ability to price compare, search inventory and transact through an app and have the item delivered to you in as little as one hour, allowing you to avoid the unwanted hassles of traffic, parking, selection or check-out lines. The common themes enabled by mobile are *connectivity, convenience, choice* and *cost* and they are combining to profoundly impact society with the lifestyle changes smartphones enable in everyday life.

The smartphone's impact on media and entertainment has been no less spectacular. Mobile devices can access virtually any piece of content ever produced including books, articles, movies, music, television shows and games. With people spending more than 3 hours per day on their devices, mobile has become, in just a few short years, the most important and strategic distribution channel for media content. People are changing the way they consume media just as they are changing the way they interact, work, shop and live their daily lives. Smartphones and tablets have led to a new behavioral norm of "multitasking" where users carry on multiple conversations simultaneously or consume and interact with media content over multiple screens. It's not unusual for people to watch a show or play a game on a tablet or television while engaged in multiple conversations about the content on one or more social media networks or messaging apps. Conversations about content range from up to the minute standings for fantasy sports to comments about an outfit worn by a celebrity on the red carpet. This new normative behavior, particularly for Millennials, has made for a more engaged viewing experience and often one that is shared or social.

With respect to media consumption, it's important to think of mobile as both a distribution device and a distribution channel rather than a locational, i.e., out of home phenomenon. Most "mobile" use is basically stationary and takes place in the home or workplace where one could easily substitute a PC or laptop. The tablet is a mobile device, but a wireless laptop on Wi-Fi is not considered to be "mobile" because the distinction is based upon the operating system that drives the device. The original value proposition of mobile to advertisers was the last mile, but while still valid, it should reflect the overall substitution effect that mobile devices are having on all media consumption whether at home, at work, while traveling or out in one's local community.

The new "mobile" platforms currently powering phones, tablets and wearables, are beginning to drive televisions, home entertainment and even autos with Apple's CarPlay and Android Auto. Don't think of a screen as linear TV, but rather think of it as a giant iPhone or Android device which will be driven by apps for news, sports, entertainment, music, games, video calls, social media, messaging, video and text feeds. In the new modern digital-distribution ecosystem, televisions should be viewed as simply another screen that will become much more versatile with long-form content generally preferred on larger screens and more short-form on mobile devices—though there will always be exceptions to both based primarily on convenience. Mobile is defined as much as an operating system driving devices or screens as it is about consumer behavior or locale. In short, smartphones and tablets are gradually replacing PCs in the home and office as users prefer the continuity, operational flexibility and the user-friendliness of mobile apps and operating systems. Behavior patterns began to change as consumers became untethered within their home and workplace environments, and perhaps more importantly, as app developers created exciting new use cases for mobile devices which in turn drove the fundamental changes in consumer behavior, attitudes and expectations.

Smartphones and tablets are also responsible for a marked increase in overall media consumption. People are watching more video, listening to more music and consuming more news and information than ever before as smartphones have become the primary personal "screen" for consumers. Online video viewing now accounts for the majority of broadband network bandwidth and is growing faster than any other category. The informal, short-hand communication style ushered in by messaging is also carrying over to media consumption. Users are demanding different content formats that more closely reflect the situational usage of their devices. Shorter content segments are accompanied by shorter-length ads, which are more compatible formats with the usage patterns of mobile devices. Another development fueling the increase in online video consumption is consumer demand for larger phones as the larger screen format is more conducive for video viewing. This behavioral shift is inexorable and will present both challenges and opportunities for content producers and distributors. Understanding mobile's impact on society manifested through the fundamental changes in consumer behavior is core to developing a successful competitive strategy in media as well as commerce and ultimately, for all other industries that serve the consumer.

YouTube has been enormously successful in creating a new norm for short-form online videos. According to a BI Intelligence poll, 81 percent of Millennials use YouTube and 79 percent of them use Netflix. Online video consumption on smartphones is the fastest growing segment in media and half the video consumption on smartphones is short form with content segments lasting five minutes or less. Messaging platforms like Snapchat, Facebook Messenger and

Twitter are also creating interesting new ways to produce and distribute short-form, online video tapping into large, networked user bases.

Mobile's impact on society is also being influenced by the way we organize and communicate through social media. According to a Pew study, in the 10-year period from 2005-2015, social media usage grew at a staggering rate from 7 to 75 percent among U.S. adults with internet access. This revolutionary tool for communicating, discovering and sharing has fundamentally changed the way people meet and interact. The essence of "tribes" has been propagated as people naturally organize around areas of common interest. Social media can be a force for good as the world witnessed with the Arab Spring, but conversely, it can also be an unwitting accomplice when used to recruit people for organizations who wish to do harm.

According to a Gallup survey, 81 percent of Americans say their smartphone is next to them during all of their waking hours and the majority of people say they check their phones multiple times per hour. These numbers are even greater for Millennials and college graduates. It's an entirely new and transformational behavioral norm that has been adopted by most Americans in just a few short years and will serve as the single most disruptive influence on media content distribution in the decade ahead.

6 | THE CONSUMER IS NOW KING: 4 C'S OF THE DIGITAL REVOLUTION

The phase "Content is King" is widely used for good reason because media and entertainment have always been hit driven businesses. Content is the core product for media companies and naturally serves as the lifeblood of a successful media company. Not surprisingly, the best content creates leverage with both distributors and advertisers and tends to be inoculated from competitive forces, which hurt profits and destroy value. Content has been a key success factor in the media value chain for decades across electronic, print and digital media as the best content not only generates more revenue, but it generally captures a greater share of the economics for its owners.

Content will always be paramount, but in today's digital world, media companies are also highly focused on how they deliver their content to maximize utility for consumers. People are consuming increasingly more content on mobile devices and want a seamless user experience. Moreover, the user experience will ultimately determine the perceived quality of the content based in part on its utility. This is a foreign concept for some content producers, but they must be mindful that media content, like consumer packaged goods, should ideally be offered to the consumer in the ways they want to consume it in order to be fully-valued. The customer dictates the rules of engagement—how do they want to consume content and what are they willing to pay for it. In short, market power is inexorably shifting towards the consumer as smartphones powered by disruptive apps are driving an on-demand economy that is becoming integral to our daily lives.

THE 4 C'S OF THE DIGITAL REVOLUTION

The key benefits that are driving consumers' rapid adoption of digital technology and services can neatly be summarized in a framework I refer to as The 4 C's: *Connectivity, Convenience, Choice and Cost*. The combination of these four effects is a new level of consumer empowerment and it has become an irreversible force that media and marketing companies ignore at their peril.

CONNECTIVITY

Connectivity is basis of the digital economy. Microsoft co-founder Paul Allen presciently discussed his vision for a "wired world" long before the internet or "World Wide Web" was widely understood. I don't know if even Paul Allen could have predicted the extent to which the world has become connected through wireless technology, mobile devices and hundreds of thousands of apps. We have truly become a connected society in the 10 years following the introduction of the iPhone and the benefits to society and individual consumers are immeasurable. Connectivity enables consumers to access instant information on virtually everything that impacts their lives. It has also trained tens of millions of users to expect access to information, content, services or people almost as quickly as they can open an app. For example, Google has become a transcendent verb synonymous with an instant answer to virtually any information or content request.

Two-thirds of Americans have smartphones today and that number is expected to rise to 90 percent by 2020. According to the Ericsson Mobility Report, smartphone subscriptions are set to more than double by 2020 with 70 percent of the world's population projected to own a smartphone. Consumers are spending more than three hours a day interacting with their phones and the time spent continues to increase as online video consumption grows. Today, people use smartphones to stay connected to family, friends and colleagues through a variety of different messaging and social networking apps. The trend of less talking and more messaging and data consumption continues to accelerate with data traffic growing at 50 percent a year with online video driving the majority of growth in data consumption.

In addition to smartphones as the fundamental tool for connectivity, wearables are a rapidly growing array of products to enhance consumers' connected experience. These products include watches and bracelets that collect and receive data to keep users connected to monitor activity, vital signs, sleep quality and communication. Wearables as an industry is expected to grow at high double-digit rates led by smartwatches which are experiencing moderate success with their early product introductions, but are expected to receive wider consumer adoption once they can function independently as another connected device without requiring a smartphone to receive, process and transmit data.

The theme of connectedness has also made its way into the home through companies like Nest, which Google acquired in 2014. For Google, Nest is the enabler of the "smart home," controlling climate, lights, appliances and security. The functionality will continue to evolve as more and more devices are connected to and enabled through the internet. The consumer's span of control over numerous devices and appliances that impact their daily lives is increasing rapidly. This higher level of connectivity both improves quality of life and raises consumers' feature-set expectations for any product they purchase in their connected digital ecosystem.

This next generation of connectivity for both enterprise and consumer is known as the "Internet of Things" or IoT and has the potential to meaningfully amplify the value proposition of connectivity. IoT is the parlance for the next big wave for consumer and commercial internet applications where wireless broadband will be used to connect and control everything from power plants to coffee makers. Municipalities, hospitals, schools, businesses and homes will all be smarter in the years ahead because of the IoT. They will be connected, share information, process data and make decisions that optimize efficiency and effectiveness. IoT is certainly worthy of a much longer discussion, but for the purpose of this book, it could present an incremental spectrum use case for radio and television broadcasters' evolving business models and perhaps more importantly, IoT can enable the personalization of the next generation of digital media distribution.

The "King" in today's media world is clearly the consumer. This unprecedented level of connectivity is empowering consumers to expect the ability to instantly access virtually any piece of content ever produced whenever they want and on any device of their choosing. News, sports, weather, entertainment, games, photos, videos, messages, music, maps and search are all expected to be on demand and mostly free in the new connected, mobile world. This is what consumers have been conditioned to expect and it's why we say the "Consumer is now King (or Queen)" in the emerging Modern Media ecosystem.

CONVENIENCE

Convenience is a key attribute and value driver to help promote the adoption of digital products and services. The Steve Jobs' led Apple was probably the first tech company to understand the importance of convenience to the user experience and aggressively employ it as a catalyst for mass consumer adoption. Their products were intuitive, easy to use and the closest thing to "plug and play" in the world of technology. This critically important attribute was deeply ingrained in the company's DNA and led to Apple's rapid penetration of the home and education segments where users did not have the benefit of corporate IT staffs to set-up and maintain hardware and software.

Consumers' desire for a convenient user experience naturally carried over from hardware and operating systems to applications and services. People consistently were drawn to user experiences that were intuitive and convenient. Likewise, they adopted new services, which were also intuitive, user friendly and offered a more convenient solution to a daily activity. Google also offered an incredibly convenient, uncluttered and simple way to instantly access information on any device and now enjoys a dominant share of the search market even as it faces multiple competitors, and does so without any real network effects like those enjoyed by social networks and messaging apps. This is a testament to Google's overall user experience, product quality and customer satisfaction that is predicated upon speed and simplicity which translate into convenience.

Other well-executed examples of this playbook include Netflix, Pandora, Instagram, Amazon, Uber, Open Table, Drop Box and Airbnb. Amazon is perhaps the best example of how a digital enterprise has been built on the consumer's desire for convenience. They have architected their business processes to make it as easy as possible to purchase goods and services from their website or app. For example, their subscription service, Amazon Prime, now has over 50 million subscribers who can simply open the app and purchase a product, literally in seconds, which is then delivered to their home that day. Better yet, Amazon can also schedule weekly or monthly deliveries custom tailored to meet their Prime member's essential needs—a wonderful service for families with infants and young children. They have made convenience a centerpiece of the consumer experience, which many people value as much or more than price.

Uber is another prime example of a convenient digital solution to address an everyday need. Its users can open the app and hire a car that arrives within a few minutes to take them anywhere they want to go without having to book a car service, hail a cab, pay the fare or calculate a tip. Similarly, Open Table takes all the hassle out of making dinner reservations, and now even Domino's makes it possible to have a pizza delivered to your home with just a couple taps on your smart phone. This level of convenience is truly unprecedented and again serves to empower the consumer who is quickly becoming accustomed to instant or on-demand access to a wide range of goods and services in the digital economy—all accessed from a smartphone.

CHOICE

Consumers have always valued choice in every product and service they purchase. They also value choice in how and where they consume products and services. In the digital world, consumers have been conditioned to expect complete access to virtually everything money can buy with no limitations based upon size, color, model, etc., as everything is accessible to them online. Digital technology has driven the dramatic expansion of choice because it ignores the physical limitations of inventory and linear distribution. The benefits are compounded as the individual selection offered by online retailers like Amazon or eBay far exceed the capabilities of a brick-and-mortar retailer, not to mention the ability of consumers to easily shop multiple sites in minutes.

One needs to look no further than Amazon to see the benefits of choice. Even in its early days as an online bookstore, it offered a full catalog of titles that could never be matched by a traditional bookstore. They have evolved this model into one of the world's most valuable companies by embracing the principles of connectivity, convenience, choice and cost to create a superior value proposition for consumers.

In an analog world, choice is naturally constrained by physical limitations. In other words, a department store has finite inventory on display, which naturally limits selection. A newspaper or magazine has a finite number of articles and images. A radio station has a finite playlist which is offered in a linear format, and a television channel has a finite list of programs which are also aired in a linear sequence. In each example, choice is far more limited than in a digital, on-demand world where there are virtually no limits to physical goods or content which has either been produced or converted to a digital format, and is individually addressable and stored in the cloud.

More choice in video content has naturally increased the amount of time people spend watching online video with growth rates accelerating due to the proliferation of OTT services and aggressive push by social networks and messaging apps to distribute online video across their networks. Online video viewing is surpassing total time spent with linear television because of the vast amount of content available combined with the increasing number of online video distribution services and devices capable of playing it. As new digital entrants emerge and analog platforms continue to migrate to digital, the ability to offer an ever-increasing selection of content will fuel a rapidly growing appetite for more content. Choice increases consumption and creates more opportunities for content producers and distributors.

COST

Perhaps the most profound impact of the digital age is the continuous improvement in efficiency throughout the value chain, which translates into lower costs for consumers. Virtually every business process that directly or indirectly leads to a transaction has been affected by digital technology. Internet distribution businesses employing digital technology have been highly effective at disintermediating brokers, agents, distributors and reps. Stockbrokers, ticket agents, travel agents, sales reps and many other professions have been largely automated by software, which in most cases is a more productive and efficient business solution. The result is lower costs, which are generally passed along to the consumer in highly competitive markets. While these digitally-driven efficiencies actually take costs out of value chain, digital technology also attacks the efficiency of markets themselves. Priceline, Expedia, Kayak, Travelocity, Trivago, Amazon, TrueCar and dozens of other sites across most every industry that sell goods and services all serve to empower the consumer with valuable information on prices. Consumers are driving market efficiency and lower costs by demanding both choice and price competition. In the new world of digital commerce, product and brand loyalty has often been subjugated to price and value. Connectivity has enabled consumers to be more informed than ever before and it has translated into more efficient markets, lower costs, lower core inflation and a higher standard of living.

Travel agents were an early causality of this phenomenon and now the industry is dominated by Priceline and Expedia, which have a combined market value of over $80 billion. According to the BLS, the number of travel agents peaked in 2000 at 125,000 and due to the rapid growth of online travel agencies (OTAs), the number of agents was cut in half by 2015 and is still declining as digital services find more ways to disrupt the legacy travel service business. Not only have travel agents been mostly eliminated, but because the booking process has been largely automated end-to-end, the airlines, hotels, rental car and cruise lines have all eliminated thousands of positions due to automated workflows.

These reduced costs have also translated into lower prices for consumers as comparative sites have made the market truly efficient. In addition to driving more efficient business processes, in the case of the travel industry, technology has also increased competition which will serve to lower costs for consumers. Airbnb has created a marketplace with over two million rooms and growing, making it much larger in accessible inventory than Marriott, Hilton and Hyatt hotels combined. Moreover, the resulting increase in lodging inventory is placing downward pressure on rates for conventional hotel companies. Uber is doing the same thing to taxis, car services and rental car companies. Digital technology impacts commerce and media in similar ways by empowering the consumer to expect instant access to all options at the lowest cost with the least amount of hassle.

In media, the consumer has also been the beneficiary of lower costs, not to mention a plethora of free product. The cost of digital movies, television shows, music, books, newspapers and magazines have never been more affordable as a percentage of median household income. Consumers enjoy more and better content at lower prices and as the economic power shifts to the consumer, they are consuming more media than ever before. The music industry has been most adversely impacted by digitally driven deflation due to streaming services, piracy and the "unbundling" of the album. Consumers can now access free music on demand from YouTube or Spotify or have custom playlists "pushed" at them by Pandora, iHeart and a host of others. Since the launch of iTunes in 2001, consumers have also been empowered to disaggregate the music bundle by buying individual songs rather than entire albums. As a result of single song unit sales, streaming services and regrettably, piracy, people are consuming more product than ever before, but the global music industry revenue has been halved from approximately $30 billion in 2000 to less than $15 billion in 2015. It's a striking example of an economic value transfer to the consumer and away from the labels and artists which the labels hope to arrest with widespread adoption of on-demand, paid subscription services like Spotify, Apple Music and Amazon.

7 | THE DISTRIBUTOR'S DILEMMA: ELIMINATING THE MIDDLEMAN

The Digital Revolution has disrupted dozens of industries including technology, retail, financial services and travel, but almost none as profoundly as media. For today's media consumers, there has never been a more exciting time to be alive. Continuous connectivity, unlimited choice, mobile convenience and lower costs are all conspiring to create an increasingly personalized media experience for consumers. Digital technology impacts virtually every aspect of our lives, but none more deeply than the way we communicate and consume media. The advent and rapid adoption of smartphones and mobile devices has transformed society and conditioned consumers to expect access to entertainment and information content whenever and wherever they wish to consume it. We have moved from a linear world where people had often scheduled their lives around the programming schedules of media companies to ensure they caught the local news and didn't miss their favorite prime-time shows, to a world where prime-time viewing is now a uniquely personal concept. The digital revolution enabled by smartphones and tablets has put the consumer squarely in charge of scheduling and curating content and not surprisingly, it is causing media and advertising companies to rethink their business models as they adjust to the new norms of consumer behavior in a mobile, connected society.

This seminal transformation of media due to the influence of technology hasn't been witnessed to this degree since the widespread adoption of the color television over 50 years ago. Media and technology have become inextricably linked, playing a significant role in people's everyday lives. As recent as the turn of the last century, media was generally thought of as the *medium* that distributed the content such as newspapers, television, radio and magazines. Moreover, the universal symbol of technology for most Americans was rooted in their personal computer. The internet was still nascent and its potential was not well understood with AOL becoming an early leader by offering access through a dial-up modem. Primitive as it may seem, it was heralded by many for enabling people to communicate via email with one another, engage in rudimentary search through AltaVista with limited e-commerce offerings and even share files including pirated media.

An early application of digital technology to media was through peer-to-peer file sharing which served to devalue content which had always been distributed through physical mediums like records, CDs, DVDs and newspapers. File sharing essentially created a virtual content store where the products were available for free, putting them at odds with content creators and distributors, as well as law enforcement. The early battles, however, set the stage for an eventual reconciliation between digital media distributors who wish to disrupt and democratize legacy analog distribution models and traditional media companies who built very profitable businesses by tightly controlling the distribution of media content.

The 4 C's of *connectivity, convenience, choice* and *cost* will work in concert to put greater pressure on distributors across the spectrum of goods and services in both the consumer and enterprise markets. The global economy is an intricate web of millions of businesses interacting with billions of customers at various points along a specific value chain with the ultimate goal of selling a product to the end user. Distribution is often an overlooked and underappreciated segment of the value chain yet in many media business models, it represents a tremendous source of value and competitive advantage.

Distributors can be enormously profitable when they have exclusive rights to products such as beer and liquor or franchise rights like those owned by car dealers who enjoy a protected status as territory-exclusive retailers. Distribution businesses without any exclusivity like supermarkets and mass market retailers are generally locked in price wars and operate with very thin profit margins and tend to rely on the need for scale to create barriers to entry which helps create leverage over vendors and suppliers.

One of the basic principles of economics is market efficiency, meaning that over time, markets have a natural tendency to gravitate towards an efficient state. Consumers will naturally act in a self-interested way to maximize value, and in a free market, producers will exploit market inefficiencies through competition wherever possible. Firms compete for profits as either new entrants in a market or as existing competitors with differentiated products and/or simply lower prices. The net effect is lower margins for existing competitors who enjoyed a temporarily "inefficient" market position. This is the basic philosophy of industrial economics, which has been influencing markets and competition for centuries.

The Digital Age, however, is transforming the concept of distribution leading to a fundamental reset in the way industries are structured. Early and obvious examples of consumer services, which have been disintermediated, are travel agents and stockbrokers. Examples that aren't as obvious are businesses that have been automated through technology like document and data management and reporting. Most enterprise software exists to automate business functions, which previously required staff and third-party vendors to execute. The drive towards optimal efficiency throughout the enterprise is leading to the elimination of a great deal of manual workflow and cumbersome business processes through digital workflow automation.

Retail is a prime example of the distributor's dilemma due to digital disruption. Moreover, it has many parallels to what is occurring in the media business as legacy and new media converge in a new paradigm we call Modern Media. Generally viewed as nonexclusive resellers, retailers are largely undifferentiated "distributors" of goods. They are mostly low net margin businesses, which have served an important role in the value chain to bring goods to market connecting producers with consumers. They bore the fixed cost of prime real estate and overhead necessary to drive and serve customer traffic, making it extremely difficult to compete on price with online retailers like Amazon, who were designed from the outset as logistics and distribution businesses. As consumer behavior shifts increasingly towards the immediacy, choice, cost and convenience of online, the brick-and-mortar retailers are becoming increasingly disadvantaged. Amazon's revenue now exceeds $125 billion dollars and is approaching one-third of WalMart's revenue—the world's largest retailer. Amazon is growing at well over 20 percent per year while WalMart's revenue has been flatlined. Not surprisingly, survey after survey reaffirms the inexorable shift of consumer attitudes and behavior in favor of online shopping at the expense of traditional brick-and-mortar retailers.

WalMart is not alone in experiencing growth challenges, as the largest department store chain, Macy's, has also been experiencing same store sales declines leading them to close unprofitable stores to defend their profit margins. As consumer behavior continues to shift towards online shopping, the challenges for retailers and their landlords will intensify. At their core, retailers will always be distributors, but will need to rethink and evolve their channel strategy. Omni-channel—the ability to operate efficiently across all retail channels—is the new strategic imperative for retailers. This book, in part, explores interesting parallels between the challenges traditional retail faces with the challenges traditional media faces—both with online competitors forcing them to reimagine their business models as distribution is transformed by digital and mobile alternatives.

THE NETWORK EFFECT

Ironically, today's digital competitors have even stronger competitive barriers derived through distribution than broadcasters or newspapers have had in the past—but for a very different reason. It's known as the "Network Effect," which simply put, means that as users of a service grow, the service becomes more valuable to its users and thus strengthens its competitive position. For example, Google Circles struggled to compete with Facebook as a mass market social network in spite of their parent company's enormous resources because most people saw little or no need to invest time in another social network when all their friends and family were already on Facebook or Instagram. Professional networks like LinkedIn also benefit in a similar way because critical mass is essential to maximize the utility of the service and fortify its competitive position.

The same is true for messaging services like Twitter, Facebook Messenger, Snapchat and WhatsApp, which all serve as communications networks for users. They all require a "counter-party" or another user in order to communicate. All of these services become more valuable to consumers as more people use them. This phenomenon serves to strengthen each of these digital distribution networks and creates powerful barriers to entry for new competitors. It also serves as a disincentive for users to switch to another network and leave most of the people they communicate with behind if they leave the network. The same is true for review sites like Yelp, where more users mean more reviews, which translate into greater utility for all users. The same is true for the auction site, eBay. Buyers and sellers both want a robust marketplace, which leads to more choice, greater liquidity and true market pricing. In short, an efficient market which delivers value to both buyers and sellers.

Uber is yet another example of a digital distribution site that has benefited greatly from the network effect. As their user base grows, their driver-base grows transforming Uber into a fully distributed, on-demand transportation service. Moreover, they have the opportunity to also disrupt the local delivery market by leveraging their existing technology and human capital to distribute physical goods such as restaurant take-out, groceries or package deliveries in addition to passengers.

Scale also has an important effect on services which become more valuable to their users as they grow even when their users don't communicate with one another. Amazon and Netflix are two examples of scale as a competitive advantage. As Amazon grows its user base and revenue, it has capital to reinvest in more distribution facilities that enables Amazon to stock more goods and deliver them faster. More choice, more convenience and lower prices make Amazon more valuable to consumers, which in turn, drives the virtuous circle of more users. Amazon is also successfully pursuing the same strategy as they do for retail in the hosted web services business competing aggressively against incumbents like Google, HP, IBM and Microsoft.

Another example of competitive advantage through scale is Netflix, which along with Amazon is one of the great disrupters of our time. In fact, Netflix is a living lesson for traditional media companies on the need to aggressively evolve their distribution models as technology creates a more attractive alternative for consumers. Everyone who is old enough remembers the fateful tale of Blockbuster, the ubiquitous video retailer that rented videocassettes and later shifted to DVDs. At its peak in 2004, Blockbuster had 60,000 employees in over 9,000 stores. A young upstart named Netflix began offering DVDs to consumers via the mail for a monthly subscription service in 1999. It rented the exact same product as Blockbuster, but did so with a different twist. It addressed the problem of late fees by allowing customers to keep the disks as long as they wanted, but they couldn't ask for more product until they returned the current titles. Netflix also changed the individual transaction model to a monthly subscription model and delivered the product directly to consumers via the mail. The benefits to the consumer were simple: No late fees, no pressure to watch and return the product and no need to venture out of the house only to find your movie sold out for the evening.

This all seems straightforward, which is why it's so hard to believe that the management at Blockbuster didn't simply copy Netflix's service early on when the first signs of cannibalization became evident. A series of focus groups with disaffected Blockbuster customers would have identified the key features consumers were looking for, as well as which features like annoying late fees left Blockbuster vulnerable to competition. Through more extensive market research, they could then identify the addressable market for the new service, quickly copy it and introduce a new direct-to-home service as another way to serve more customers by the "trusted" leader in home entertainment. Consumers were demanding online ordering, mail delivery and no late fees, and Netflix was given a long runway to build and maintain a competitive advantage that should have been fleeting at best.

If the decision not to act was made to protect the late fee income, it turned out to be a "bet the ranch" decision that failed. Blockbuster had the brand, the customer data, the retail locations, the relationships with the studios, and the distribution facilities necessary to create an online offering delivered via direct mail or held for pick-up at the store. In fact, it would have been much easier for them to execute this strategy than it was for Netflix. In short, they believed in the durability of their own business model too much and it prevented them from objectively studying a disrupter and responding aggressively with a copycat (or superior) offering. Ironically, it was rumored that Blockbuster was offered the opportunity to acquire Netflix in 2000 for $50 million and they turned it down. Today Netflix has a market capitalization of almost $50 billion and Blockbuster has since been broken-up and sold in bankruptcy.

Netflix is an excellent example of a new company entering a market with a strategy to disrupt the market leader's business model. It was clearly effective against Blockbuster and other competitors like Hollywood Video, but Netflix was not content to rest on their initial success. In another brilliant move, Netflix preemptively disrupted themselves when they begin offering a streaming video service and phased-out their core DVD mail distribution business. The writing was on the wall for physical media when Apple began streaming digital audio in order to offer digital music downloads through iTunes in 2001. The result was devastating for the retail music industry, which was approximately $30 billion in global sales in 2000, but was roughly halved by 2015 with downloads and streaming revenue unable to replace the rapid decline of physical album and singles sales. Disruption of the analog (physical) distribution channel and widespread unauthorized use left the recorded music industry—like the newspaper industry—unable to protect their intellectual property and over time, content become widely available without a direct transaction. Consequently, many consumers no longer value what they can legally access for free through streaming and on-demand services. Digital download sales along with the combined subscription and ad-supported revenue models have not come close to recapturing lost revenue from the highly controlled and profitable legacy distribution channels. In contrast and early on, the television and motion picture studios took a much more aggressive approach to piracy and thus have maintained the perceived value of their product.

It took several years, however, before the team at Netflix felt the technology was robust and reliable enough to offer digital video streaming as an alternative to its mail order video business, and they announced a deal with Epix in 2010 rather than play catch-up to a competitor like Apple. Netflix did with aplomb what Blockbuster had failed to do—they leveraged an existing market position and customer relationships to evolve their business model following a technology-led paradigm shift to digital streaming. They elbowed themselves into a highly profitable industry with an innovative business model, then turned it on its head to catch the next wave of innovation through video streaming. Their success has invited a raft of competitors including Amazon, Hulu, Apple, Sony and others. The market opportunity is enormous so several competitors will flourish. The early success of these entrants enable them to build scale which creates natural barriers to entry for yet another new wave of competitors. Additionally, it can serve as a disincentive for users to switch to another network without the user base of family, friends and colleagues following specific shows and all regularly being introduced to new content on familiar networks.

REGULATORY PROTECTIONS

Businesses that have benefited from protected positions that serve as barriers to new competitors are an exception to this rule. The attractive profit margins from these businesses are due to various factors including: regulation, intellectual property rights, capital investment, network effects and franchise agreements. The media business is comprised of many sub-industries of distributors who enjoy one or more of these protections, many of which are or will be in jeopardy because of the proliferation of digital disrupters. The internet is a free, ubiquitous digital distribution channel that will enable new competitors to disintermediate many existing distribution businesses and reduce profitability in many others. Media distributors and content producers will both be impacted by this phenomenon as consumers adopt new platforms and shift their consumption behavior.

The media industries benefiting from regulation include broadcasters, satellite, wireless and cable companies. Regulated by the FCC, these businesses have historically been protected against new entrants enabling them to operate high-margin businesses in an oligopoly-type industry structure. Cable television, which is also regulated by local municipalities, has essentially competed as a near-monopoly for video and broadband distribution for decades with tangential competition from satellite and wireline phone companies. Broadcasters, both radio and television, own and distribute content and have greater insulation against digital distribution, but each for different reasons. Radio will continue to rely on its broadcast distribution for in-car listening well through the next decade and likely beyond, whereas television broadcasters have long relied on cable and satellite distribution for over 90 percent of their viewing. Broadcast television is becoming increasingly dependent upon the pay TV bundle with almost a quarter of their revenue coming indirectly from pay television subscribers in the form of retransmission fees. This newfound revenue stream is under pressure however, as the number of traditional pay TV subscribers declines in addition to the increasing demands by television networks to be compensated for the network programming that local affiliates are essentially "reselling" to the MVPDs, including cable and satellite providers.

The local cable companies are video distributors that enjoy franchise status from local municipalities. Cable TV companies were granted franchises in the 1970s to build-out the local networks. They were then required to wire homes in a connected network through which they would distribute video. This "pipe" into the home has since been leveraged to distribute broadband to the home, which now represents the fastest growing product for cable companies. The incumbent cable companies are protected by both franchise rights from local municipalities, as well as the tremendous cost for a new entrant to "overbuild" their footprints. The latter is being challenged however, as new entrants including Google Fiber are introducing service in select markets across the country with ultra-high speed broadband for a better consumer experience at comparable prices to cable. While growing rapidly, it's still a very small business and is not viewed as an immediate threat to the large cable companies who dominate the market for in-home broadband. As network owners and distributors, cable companies already sell the next generation of distribution and by creating bundled offerings, they should continue to enjoy a very profitable position as video and broadband distributors direct to consumers. Competition will increase, particularly for video program offerings, so margin pressure is likely to intensify in this segment of their business. Longer term, expect a multitude of offerings from broadcast and cable networks, as well as local broadcasters, which will put continued pressure on the large pay television bundle, slowly shifting the revenue mix for MVPDs towards broadband and home services.

MEDIA DISTRIBUTORS AT RISK

The record labels are a prime example of a media distribution business which has been materially disrupted by digital technology. Labels have been hurt through digital-enabled piracy as well as by the disaggregation of the bundle (album) as single song downloads cannibalized the highly profitable sales of albums. Longer term, the labels next existential threat will come from the most bankable artists and their management companies who have the newfound leverage to potentially circumvent the labels by going directly to radio, streaming services, SiriusXM and digital music stores as well as continuing to deal directly with concert promoters. Recorded music was the first entertainment medium to be disrupted by digital distribution and the threat continues almost two decades later as artists and managers aggressively work to capture greater value for their art in the face of declining revenues while their popularity as well as the consumption of their music is on the rise.

Likewise, book publishers will also face increasing pressure in the retail channel, but unlike music, the physical book, both hardback and paperback are still relevant with consumers, representing about three-quarters of unit sales volume. While still material, e-books sales have leveled off. Today, consumers are much more likely to download a song than they are to download a digital book. The retail channel for books, however, continues to shift online with brick-and-mortar retail now accounting for just 20 percent of book sales by volume. In addition to Amazon and Barnes & Noble Online, retail heavyweights WalMart and Target also offer a full selection of hard and paperback books through their websites, offering greater selection and lower prices which closely follow the 4 C's framework for digital disruption.

Eventually, the brick-and-mortar channel will evolve away from a traditional retail sales operation and will transition to a more of a communal place to leisurely browse, which is more akin to a university coffee house with a more limited selection of new books. Ironically, Amazon recently opened their first brick-and-mortar bookstore after having disintermediated thousands of similar operations over the last 20 years. Amazon likely views the dearth of local bookstores as potentially harmful to keeping consumers interested in buying and reading books. There has always been a certain social and intellectual appeal to being well-read and displaying a certain facileness with literature. Led by Amazon, publishers and retailers have a vested interest in keeping both books and reading a high priority for consumers of all ages.

Digital technology was initially disruptive to book retailers and now that the die has effectively been cast, the next phase of disruption is targeting the book publishers. Self-publishing of print, e-books and audio books is democratizing book publishing to a greater degree than music or film. According to Publisher's Weekly, the Big 5 book publishers accounted for just 16 percent of the e-books on Amazon's Best Seller list. The ability to self-publish both electronic and print books in conjunction with up to 75 percent of sales going through an online retail channel is meaningfully shifting leverage from the publisher to the content creator because they now have viable alternatives to traditional book publishers. With low or negative growth, traditional publishers have the burden of high fixed costs, which need to be covered by a shrinking share of marketable titles. Look for consolidation long term and fewer imprints in the near term. Moreover, smart publishing houses will embrace the trend and disrupt themselves with new entrants in the self-publishing space such as Simon and Schuster's Archway. Self-publishing, independent publishing and on-demand printing are all beneficiaries of digital technology and are disrupting the highly mature book publishing industry which has been around for well more than a century.

Pure play online music services including Pandora, Spotify, Apple Music, Deezer and Rhapsody are distributors of digital audio and collectively, they generate billions in revenue yet are losing money with no end in sight. They are all challenged due to a combination of industry structure and content costs driven by digital copyrights for songwriters and performers. Consumers have not yet embraced subscription-based music streaming as they've done with video because they've been conditioned that premium music content is available on demand for free with inserted ads. This naturally limits the addressable market for paid subscribers and negatively impacts the perceived value of the subscription offering. The existence of several standalone digital music distributors is perpetuated by public and private capital markets which continue to fund companies burning cash with the promise that increased scale and competitive attrition will make the bet pay off. The problem with that thesis is that scale isn't a panacea for business models with high customer acquisition costs and little or no operating leverage due to a high variable cost structure, which means profitability improves only marginally with increased sales volume.

Expect consolidation in the space as both Apple and Google offer subscription services through their iTunes and YouTube platforms running on their iOS and Android mobile operating systems. In addition, expect Amazon to continue to ramp their music service through their Prime offering. All three have enormous user bases throughout the world replete with user data to personalize the user experience. Similar to the payments processing business, they are in a position to sustain significant structural operating losses if necessary to fortify their respective positions as online content distributors. As distribution for media, commerce and financial services continues to move online, scale will be essential, leaving Amazon, Google, Facebook and Apple with a collective competitive advantage which is currently playing-out in media distribution, advertising and commerce with payments being the next to follow.

Newspapers are another form of content distribution that is also being disrupted by the large digital distributors. It began with Craigslist as a "distributor" of classified ads, which offered an online, free alternative and thus effectively neutralized this profitable revenue stream for newspaper publishers. Google, Yahoo, Facebook and Twitter have served as the primary distributors of online news content through linking stories of interest to individual users. The majority of the online news consumption originates from one of the primary digital distributors and is then routed to the publisher's sites for consumption. Facebook is moving towards a "walled garden" approach with Instant Articles, a feature that eliminates linking as publisher content is served directly from Facebook. The value to the user is "convenience" because they don't have to wait on load times and they remain in the Facebook app. For the publishers, it's déjà vu all over again. They cede their power as a branded "distributor" of the content they pay to produce with the promise of increased revenue yield per story due to Facebook's enormous user base and data. To date, neither the hypotheses of increased yield per article, nor conversion of increased traffic to paid subscribers has been proven, but publishers continue to chase traffic in the hope of finding a viable business model.

The essence of the distributor's dilemma is the obsolescence of business models that were predicated upon physical barriers to entry fostered in an analog world. In a connected world, content production and distribution become democratized and streamlined. Large online distributors in both media and commerce are obviating the need for the legacy structure of an intricate web of middlemen who previously stood between producers and consumers. A fundamental distribution channel restructuring is underway and will cause significant disruption in the media space as traditional and new media converge over the next decade.

8 | MODERN MEDIA BRANDS ARE MULTIPLATFORM AND DEVICE-AGNOSTIC

Consumers are quickly evolving to view mediums as simply different screens rather than different experiences, and they are increasingly becoming agnostic and utilitarian as to which screen they're consuming content on. They are engaging more with the content rather than the medium because the medium of choice is driven by the user's lifestyle needs at that particular moment. In other words, they watch shows on whichever device is most convenient for them at the time they choose to view the content. The experience is no longer device-centric, but rather content-centric as consumers are constantly connected to at least one screen and the experience between screens is becoming continuous as they demand the ability to consume their favorite content anytime and on any device.

This technology-enabled behavioral change is leading to more overall consumption of media including video, audio, text and images. Television viewing was generally thought of as an activity people did while at home, usually in the evening during "prime-time" and for live sports on weekends. The linear nature of the content delivery also conditioned viewers to schedule the rest of their activities around the shows they wanted to watch by "appointment." Television viewing was also a communal experience because the family had to conform to the network's schedule and with generally one nice television set in every home, it necessarily encouraged a communal or family viewing experience. This phenomenon has largely disappeared in the 21st century household due to the availability of on-demand content which takes the rigidity out of viewing habits, empowering the viewer to program their own viewing experience.

Another important behavioral effect of technology is the personalization of content that is enabled by on-demand services, as well as the proliferation of devices that enables virtually every individual to customize their own unique content experience. A young colleague in my office had an hour-long commute to work each day and was a huge fan of "Game of Thrones." Working long hours with a young family, he didn't have time to sit back and watch it on his big screen television set, so he would watch it on his iPhone during his commute in stop-and-go traffic by positioning his smartphone on the dash enabling him to keep up with the series. While this is obviously not an advisable way to consume video content, it's very illustrative of the new attitude of Millennials towards content. They are increasingly screen agnostic and will stay current with a widening array of television shows by consuming them on a tablet or smartphone in a way that complements their lifestyle rather than altering their lifestyle to conform to linear content offerings with live sports being the primary and obvious exception.

The widespread adoption of social media has also morphed media consumption into a multitasking activity where content is consumed and simultaneously shared and discussed with a larger community of engaged consumers. Television viewing has transformed from a family activity to highly personal activity where a family of three could be in the living room with the television on and two of the three family members are watching something different on iPads or smartphones while carrying on a group conversation on a messaging app or following what the much larger community is saying on Snapchat or Twitter. The same three family members are in the same room with the large screen TV on, but they each have very individual viewing experiences.

Go into college dorm rooms and you'll be hard-pressed to find a television set—or many textbooks for that matter. Laptops, tablets and smartphones are the devices that young people are using to communicate through social media, read books, consume news, listen to music, play games and watch videos. Media is becoming a seamless experience across devices rather than a segmented activity around a particular medium, with content and advertising specifically designed for that unique experience. Video is not a communal experience for Millennials, but rather a social experience using multiple connected devices to interact with other people through social media platforms, often while simultaneously consuming and even producing content.

In direct contrast to McLuhan's famous axiom from the 1960s, the *message* is the now the medium rather than the other way around because the message transcends the medium as consumers demand continuity as they move from screen to screen depending upon their location and activities. Technology has permitted this kind of unprecedented flexibility to access content wherever and whenever a consumer may choose. The traditional media consumption patterns are being radically changed. A favorite television program which required appointment viewing each Wednesday night at 9 p.m. on the couch in your family room is now just as easily being watched on a smartphone while sitting in a doctor's office waiting room at 1 p.m. the next day. It's a significant behavioral shift that is enabled by technology and driven by a fundamental shift in media away from linear content platforms including channels and networks to on-demand distribution platforms like Netflix, Hulu and Amazon. The ability to transition across multiple screens and platforms is also creating a powerful new model for franchise media brands. The notion of a channel as a linear offering of programs is being replaced over time by apps which are brand-centric and offer related content across multiple online platforms including video, audio, newsfeeds, games, e-commerce, messaging and social. Multiplatform content offerings represent the future for several reasons.

First, they take full advantage of modern technology which is driving consumers to be platform and device agnostic. The mediums are now audio, video and text and are interchangeable across all screens including televisions, PCs, tablets and smartphones. Again, they're all just screens and over time they will look, act and function much the same. Second, consumers engage with multiple devices while consuming content. Short attention spans require more ways to simultaneously keep consumers engaged with a piece of content because it can enhance the user experience and create deeper levels of engagement, which are both essential elements for building a loyal fan base. Third, advertisers also understand that people are changing the way they interact with media and are laser-focused on marketing plans that create greater levels of engagement with target consumers. It's a virtuous circle where technology has untethered the consumer, creating boundless options on how and what content can be consumed. Barriers to entry for content creators and distributors are falling, causing a hypercompetitive environment in what has traditionally been a relatively staid media ecosystem. Experimentation with new formats and integrations is leading to a measurable increase in the levels of engagement with consumers which in turn, is attracting the attention of consumer marketers who are under pressure to provide greater ROI for their marketing spend.

ESPN and Disney are two leading media brands that are successfully executing a multiplatform strategy at scale, but building it with a traditional media foundation. From their signature parties at the Super Bowl to their College Game Day live broadcasts, ESPN, as an entertainment brand, does an excellent job of connecting with fans on location, giving them one more touch point to build deeper levels of engagement with the venerable brand. The ESPN brand began as a linear cable channel and added not only broadcast and satellite radio, but a magazine, live events and a major commitment to interactive digital sites and apps. Their digital offerings include audio and video streaming, on-demand content, newsfeeds and interactive commentary by their talent. The online experience is video-rich and designed to be interactive and encourages content sharing through social media and messaging platforms. The various analog and digital components are neatly integrated to provide a compelling user experience designed to maximize engagement with the brand's rich trove of sports content. Sports is a very crowded market with NBC, CBS, FOX and Turner all gunning for ESPN's estimated $50 billion market value and to date, ESPN has made it difficult for any of their erstwhile competitors to gain a real toehold in the all-sports cable network battle.

As strong as ESPN is, its parent Disney was the original multiplatform media and entertainment brand with theme parks, movies, theatre, cartoons, television, books, records and toys. Each of these elements was carefully crafted to support the brand of Disney and its franchise brands including Mickey Mouse, Snow White and Cinderella. Disney has since expanded its stable of franchise brands through the strategic acquisitions of Pixar, Marvel Comics and Lucas Films, creating a robust pipeline of new opportunities to repeat and innovate the playbook. Disney is now replete with major franchise brands including: "Star Wars," "Spiderman," "The Avengers," "Toy Story" and "Frozen." The company has a proven formula for extracting value from these franchise brands through an integrated offering of multimedia content distributed across several channels, as well as experiential through theme parks and merchandise through licensing agreements sold through retail, online and at Disney attractions.

Disney is the most powerful, global platform model in media and serves as the template for the strategic shift to multiplatform, digitally driven media content and distribution businesses. The Walt Disney Company has consistently driven profitability by extending their franchise brands across media platforms and branded merchandise. The goal of multiplatform brands is to create multiple touch points with fans to strengthen the bond and create more opportunities to leverage the relationship through media, live events and commerce.

Disney is bringing this successful analog strategy squarely into the digital age with their introduction of Disney Life in Europe. Disney life bundles books, music, animated and live action films. It is an on-demand service distributed through an app to stream its content directly to consumers. The innovative offering is not yet viable in the U.S. because of their existing agreements with U.S. distributors for film and television, which may preclude certain digital distribution options.

Another example of a true multiplatform, modern media brand is Bloomberg. It's a global information brand which boasts one of the largest news gathering operations in the world. The business began as an information and messaging service for bond traders looking to gain an edge through more timely information on quotes and trades. Traders also valued the Bloomberg terminal's messaging feature as a convenient way to monitor and participate in market chatter. This feature was also instrumental in creating a network effect for the Bloomberg Terminal as the service grew to be the largest on Wall Street. The more users on the network, the more valuable it became to the rest of the user community.

As growth matured, Bloomberg developed a strategy to fortify its market position. As digital technology enabled increased competition for both communication and information, Bloomberg sought to create more perceived value in the terminal subscription—which represents the vast majority of their revenue—by aggressively building a global news organization with television, radio, digital, print media and live events. The Bloomberg platforms are highly integrated and purposed to reinforce the brand by providing a high quality, focused user experience for both the professional user and business-oriented consumer market. The various platforms also smartly reinforce the value of the "Terminal" which drives the company's revenue model.

Activision, Vice and BuzzFeed are digital media brands which are building multiplatform brands by adding traditional platforms like linear cable and live events. Activision Blizzard, the largest publisher of video games recently announced the creation of film and television units to build multiplatform content assets for its hit video game brands like "Call of Duty." The games have a large and loyal fan base that will likely follow the brand and its characters from the video game to the big screen. The strategy is straight from Disney's playbook and if successfully executed, will provide an incremental revenue stream for the company as it recruits creative talent and bids for the next big hit to leverage into a multiplatform franchise brand.

Another poignant example targeting Millennial men is Vice Media. The acclaimed multiplatform brand, which counts Disney and Hearst as investors, is a digital media company, which got its start as an underground magazine in Toronto. The counterculture DNA of founder Shane Smith remains very much alive in the company as it has matured into a multiplatform, digital media and marketing services company targeting Millennial men. Vice has been at the vanguard of creating custom, sponsored content that often appears as native advertising in the company's content offerings. They have touted this as one of their key strengths in reaching young men with engaging messages that drive results for marketers.

The success of this model is closely watched, particularly the success with young males whom consumer marketers find to be hard to reach and even harder to engage. Vice is continuing its expansion across media platforms with its recent acquisition of A&E's H2 linear cable channel, which Vice has rebranded as Viceland. The move demonstrates the need for multiple platforms to reach a broader audience and perhaps more importantly, the continued strategic and economic value of the linear pay television ecosystem. The irony is not lost that one of the most successful digital media companies is making a significant investment in a traditional, linear cable channel.

BuzzFeed is another example of a digital media company, which started narrowly and like Vice, is also expanding into a multiplatform brand with online video and motion pictures. The company originally built its brand on the clever curation of third-party content that went viral through sharing on popular social networks. This tactic has been very successful in driving traffic and ad dollars. Similar to Vice, BuzzFeed is also widely praised for its popular native advertising format where sponsor's advertisements appear in the form of content that flows organically with content being served. The goal of native advertising or sponsored content is to make the advertising message seem more intuitive and less intrusive in an effort to engage consumers with the sponsor's brand to help drive higher ROI.

Multiplatform speaks to the legacy structure of individual mediums including television, radio and print. The structural siloes separating these mediums continue to fade with the inevitable transition to digitally distributed media. Television, radio and print are also becoming video, audio and text and will co-exist seamlessly on an app as a multimedia experience on a unified platform.

A successful execution of this strategy will require an intuitive, not forced integration that enhances the user experience. Moreover, the integrated components should be designed to support a simultaneous, multiscreen engagement enabling users to consume, share and interact with both the brand and sponsored content on multiple devices.

The new standard for multiplatform media companies will draw from the innovative practices of these companies as well as others and create additional features that are particular to their brands. Success will not be based upon a standard template, but rather on a constantly evolving set of fundamentals combined with the latest capabilities enabled by technology. This type of approach will inform and shape both the content and advertising offerings of successful multiplatform brands.

9 | DATA IS THE NEW CREATIVE

The advertising business is being disrupted even more violently than the media business which serves it. The major ad holding companies as well as the independents are witnessing record high client turnover as marketers face mounting pressure to justify ad spend in a low-growth environment. CMOs are being influenced by the digital cognoscenti to shift ever more of their budgets to programmatic online video because of superior targeting and measurement. What is often left out of the calculus, however, is the significant "leakage" to digital middlemen who insert themselves between the marketer and the publisher. Moreover, the inability to reach large audiences with a consistent message delivered in a supportive context is also often overlooked in the digital debate. Digital marketing has been an industry in constant transition with thousands of new entrants devising ways to insert themselves into the value chain, but similar to the inevitable convergence in media, the advertising business will also find its "modern" model through the convergence of legacy agencies and advertising technology (ad tech) platforms, and importantly, scale will be a determinant factor.

Traditionally, the legacy ad agency creative model was based around a creative team which surfaced ideas, debated concepts, and then relied on focus groups, concept testing, anecdotal feedback and sheer gut to create and refine a campaign which was then presented to the client for sign-off. Concept in hand, the broader agency team would then work to execute the creative strategy across media platforms as outlined in the media plan. The inherent risk with this approach is that great advertising, like hit records or box office sensations, is rooted in the art form of storytelling. Advertising is also very much a hit driven business, and as with records, movies, TV shows or video games, it's always difficult to predict a hit with market research. This creative uncertainty also contributes to the age-old marketer's complaint that "half their ad dollars don't work, but they don't know which half."

The legacy creative model is now being reimagined through a new data-driven approach, employing digital ad technology that now allows marketers to iterate on creative strategies with real-time feedback. Data and analytics certainly don't replace creative storytelling, but they do afford marketers the ability to take creative risks without having to go "all in" on any given campaign. Furthermore, instead of coalescing around one primary creative execution, marketers are now employing multiple creative executions with more precise targeting and more personalized messaging. The data and real-time analytics are transforming both the creative process and media execution including targeting, planning and buying.

The promise and inevitability of digital media is to make virtually every piece of content available to consumers whenever they want it, wherever they want it and on whatever device they would like to consume it. Likewise, the promise of digital advertising is to dynamically serve the ideal creative message to an individually targeted consumer at the most opportune time to engage them with a message that is optimized for the form of the device (or devices) the consumer is currently using. Moreover, the dynamic ad serving process also ensures that ad copy is optimized for the specific situational characteristics including location, time of day and even current weather conditions.

AD TECH ACCELERATES SHARE SHIFT

The aspirations for highly personalized digital content and advertising were in fact, unthinkable when the iPhone was first launched, but rapid innovations in mobile computing and ad technology combined with consumer's broad adoption of social media platforms have conspired to make seemingly quixotic concepts largely inevitable. Large data sets and the increasingly sophisticated applications to capture and analyze them are the primary drivers of the technology responsible for revolutionizing digital advertising. "Ad Tech" as it's known, is a highly complex web of services and applications that connect advertisers, also known as marketers, with media companies, also known as publishers.

The majority of revenue in the media industry is generated through the sale of advertising with the bulk of the non-ad revenue coming from pay television subscriptions. U.S. ad spend is expected to reach $190 billion in 2016 with digital accounting for just over $60 billion. However, by 2020, the U.S. market is expected to reach $215 billion with digital exceeding $100 billion. Thus in the five years between 2016-2020, the total U.S. ad market is expected to grow by $25 billion, but digital will grow by over $40 billion implying negative growth of $15 billion by non-digital media. The implications of this accelerating share shift are alarming for traditional media's core ad business, particularly newspapers and most types of magazines where the losses will be greatest both on a nominal and percentage basis.

Hardest hit in the print segment are newspapers, which will continue to experience revenue declines, sliding to approximately $14 billion in 2020, down from a peak of $50 billion in 2005. Retail, national and classified newspaper advertising will all continue to fall at double-digit rates per year while digital ad revenue will continue to grow. Radio and television broadcasters will also continue to see pricing erosion in their core advertising business, but will be offset to varying degrees by their online product offerings as the shift to digital accelerates through advances in optimization, targeting and automation. Each of the traditional media segments (television, radio, newspaper and magazines) will have a significant and growing digital business by 2020, but success will vary company by company depending upon their respective digital strategies and perhaps, more importantly, based upon their level of execution as they move beyond their core competencies and product offerings. Look for a great deal of experimentation and iteration over the next few years by traditional media companies as they develop integrated digital ad products and present more solution-based, integrated offerings to their clients. Fast followers will invariably imitate competitor's successful strategies, driving the need for continued innovation in their go-to-market strategies.

The ad markets are in the early innings of a profound change as marketers move inexorably towards planning a majority of their ad spend in digital media as we enter the next decade. On its face, one might argue that the advertising industry has already undergone profound changes to keep up with the emerging digital technologies when in reality, the converse is true. The major ad holding companies are in the early stages of transforming their legacy businesses with many acquiring digital agencies to enable them to respond more quickly to their client's immediate needs. This approach is not without risk because oftentimes, these "acquisition-hires" are difficult to integrate and not properly acculturated with the new employees and skillsets getting lost in a large organization already sensitive to impending turf battles. For ad agencies, truly embracing a digital culture requires a transformative approach to strategy, creative, planning and buying. Teams need to be reimagined and turf battles need to be addressed head-on and decisively resolved. It's hard work and will take several years but the alternative is to be left behind. A parallel construct is playing out in a similar manner with traditional media companies as well. Ironically, both industries are well-positioned to compete successfully in the digital world, but a significant number of seemingly viable competitors in each industry will be unable to move fast enough, ceding relevance as the disrupters work to take advantage of stasis and capture valuable market share and goodwill.

DYNAMIC ADVERTISING

The future of advertising is dynamic personalization and should prove to be a material game-changer for media companies, advertisers and consumers alike. Media companies will be able to sell smarter impressions, which are worth more when systematically matched with the optimal buyer. Advertisers will be able to buy more efficiently and expect higher conversion rates due to better audience targeting and creative optimization. Consumers also win because they will be exposed to more relevant ads, which will ultimately make for a more enjoyable content experience. To effect the process, marketers will demand the ability to serve an optimized message to an individually targeted prospect at the most opportune time to maximize engagement and drive activation or purchase. This may sound like "internet speak" but it's rapidly becoming the everyday lexicon of modern marketers and more importantly, it's what they expect to accomplish with an increasingly larger share of their marketing dollars with each passing year. The technology of 1-to-1 addressability is very straightforward: when you're consuming content on an addressable device, chances are good that marketers can serve you "smart" ads that you should find more relevant than in a non-addressable environment.

Pre-digital, ad targeting was based upon a general knowledge of an audience as estimated by Nielsen for television and radio, along with the ABC (Audit Bureau of Circulation) for newspapers and magazines. The ratings services would estimate audience sizes with cross-tabulated data on age and gender. Qualitative datasets that gave more insight into the audience through dimensions like income, education, preferences and purchase intent were considered to be breakthrough tools in their day and were adopted by various marketers to help differentiate media offerings.

The majority of dollars placed in electronic media, however, have been planned and negotiated based upon the audience ratings data which is used as "currency" with the standard metric of GRPs or gross rating points. This is the protocol employed for spot television and local cable, as well as network television, the cable nets and all broadcast radio. Absent a better alternative, the data marketers have been using to invest tens of billions of their client's ad dollars each year is little more than a rudimentary estimate of the number of viewers or listeners for a given time period tabulated by age and gender. As the industry standard, Nielsen ratings have served as the currency to help make a market between buyers and sellers of advertising, but in its current form, it lacks the sophistication that marketers are increasingly demanding in the digital age, including more robust audience data and analytics, as well as the ability to transact programmatically with real-time bidding.

Today's marketers are aggressively looking for every possible edge to eliminate waste in order to gain efficiency in their marketing spend. When buying mass-targeted campaigns, marketers are paying for impressions which are invariably run multiple times against individual consumers who have little or no chance of becoming viable prospects. Return on Investment (ROI) is the Holy Grail metric for marketers and thanks to ever more sophisticated business intelligence applications, it's becoming easier to track results in real time. Increased transparency is causing marketers to obsess over their ROI data because it's their most important performance metric. For marketers, there are three principal levers to improve ROI: targeting, media mix and creative.

In the Mad Men generation of the 1960s, the primary focus was on breakthrough creative. Media choices were relatively few in an analog-only world with television, radio, newspaper and magazines capturing the bulk of ad spend. Television was widely used for prime-time mass reach and during daytime to reach primarily "stay-at-home moms," which fueled the creation of the Daytime Soap Operas sponsored by the large consumer products companies like P&G and Unilever. Radio was used heavily in drive times to reach commuters with newspapers capturing the price-item advertising for retail, grocery and auto along with their cash-cow classifieds. Breakthrough creative drove the culture of Madison Avenue with media buying strategies comparatively less complex and basically assumed because there simply weren't that many choices to reach Americans and behavior and culture were far more homogenous and predictable than it is today.

DATA DRIVES TARGETING AND MEDIA MIX

The sophistication and availability of data has followed somewhat of a "hockey stick" growth curve from the Mad Men generation to today because the granularity of the data in the 1960s wasn't appreciably different than the data in the 1990s. For over four decades, ad buys were made on audience estimates from meters or diaries with basic cross-tabulation of age and gender or "demos" such as 18-49 adults or 25-54 women. In fact, it wasn't until the relaunch of Web 2.0 following the dotcom crash that consumer adoption of the web began to take off, first with browsers, then followed by portals, search, social and mobile. The mass adoption of the internet including search and social media has indirectly created enormous data sets across all industries commonly referred to as "big data." Information is continuously collected on consumers and businesses that marketers are eager to exploit in their quest for more efficient targeting and higher ROI.

THE CONSUMERS UNWITTING ROLE IN MARKETING DATA

The two principal types of data which marketers use to improve targeting are "core" and "derivative," and it is useful to understand them both. Though they are often disparate data sets, they can be powerful tools when combined to help marketers link ad buys with product sales.

Core data is essentially empirical data or a series of inputs before any analysis is completed to develop additional or "derivative" insights. Core data by itself, is very helpful to marketers because it includes basic demographic or census data such as age, gender, marital status, children, income, education and occupation. It also includes consumer information such as home owner-ship, vehicle registration, as well as other consumer products purchases that you may have volunteered when completing forms for product registrations, surveys or warranty cards. It's a safe bet that most all information you provide is aggregated and sold to marketers and data companies according to each of their individual privacy statements which most people don't take the time to read. This type of consumer data is captured not only by purchases, but also activities like sporting events, charities, fairs, festivals, amusement parks and resorts. Again, basically any forum where you are asked for registration information is likely to become a set of core data linked to you as a consumer, which is why it's important to read privacy policies carefully and exercise your right to opt out if don't wish your data to be shared.

Core data is collected both online and offline with the online collection done primarily through the "cookies" embedded on your computer. Cookies track your every move on the web including what sites you visit, how long you visit and which pages you're spending time with, but they are not used in mobile operating systems. They are essentially a file that is loaded on your computer, with some cookies being temporary while others are more permanent, meaning they will reside on your computer until you delete them. Embedded cookies are what enable you to move from page to page within a website to store items in a virtual shopping cart while browsing a site. Marketers can, however, place cookies on your computer from sites you've never visited through ad networks which serve as re-sellers of third-party online advertising. In short, consumers unwittingly give marketers a treasure trove of information on a daily basis that is used as data for selling and serving smarter ads.

The ability of large ad networks to infiltrate devices understandably has many consumers nervous about privacy. With the shift to mobile, cookies dis-tributed through browsers are becoming less effective as mobile usage is shifting toward apps. This is making it much tougher for marketers to track usage across mobile apps and devices for the average consumer than with a desktop browser.

Core data by itself, represents an incomplete picture of individual consumers, but with the help of sophisticated data modeling, marketers can employ educated inferences to better identify audiences for virtually any product or service. The value of this data to marketers is the ability to create truly personalized marketing campaigns, which require the one-to-one addressability of digital media. Specific analytics can now be applied to big data sets to provide marketers with the tools to measure performance, including which marketing channels and creative treatments outperformed on activation or conversion. The product of these analytics are known as *derivative data*, an exciting science that analyzes multiple data sets looking for correlations that can be predictive of consumer behavior. Data science has become big business for the dozens of companies competing in the electronic data processing space where scale is required to both purchase and analyze massive amounts of data in order to generate relevant insights of value to their customers. Predicative insights can be helpful to spot emerging trends for product launches or acquisitions or conversely, areas for disinvestment. For marketers, derivative data is a nuanced way of amplifying core data to paint a richer picture of individual consumers to provide guidance on likely purchase behavior.

Consumers are akin to a mosaic where each individual tile represents the products and services they consume. Most discrete transactions are not disclosed to marketers other than the obvious data that belongs to merchants you purchase goods from. For example, if you are a Millennial male, and buy a television set from an online retailer, data analytics will process that you are interested in consumer electronics, shop online and are likely to be a candidate for gaming console, digital camera or OTT subscription video service.

Facebook has created more of a "front door" way to capture a vast array of data by inviting users to log in to mobile apps using Facebook credentials. It is viewed by many Facebook users as a convenient way to be identified and take advantage of a more personalized experience while in a third-party app. This innocuous convenience for the user is an extremely valuable asset for

Facebook as it captures even more data about the user while they are away from the Facebook environment to create a richer profile which, in turn, helps them execute more targeted campaigns through their exchanges. Facebook is becoming one of the most powerful data technology companies in the world with rich data on the majority of populations across the globe. They are also smartly providing tool kits for marketers to optimize campaigns for both targeting and creative. Facebook is also extending their utility by providing marketers with the ability to target "lookalike" audience segments drawing upon their vast database of user profiles and behavioral data to find strong correlations and a resulting match for high value prospects to sell incremental smart impressions to marketers and increasingly, these impressions are in the form of video ads.

Borne out of these data-driven targeting technologies are the essential tools for retargeting which helps marketers follow prospects around the web in an effort to continue marketing to them once they've shown an interest. If you've ever searched for a car, hotel or dress shirt, you've undoubtedly had the searched brand "follow" you around to the various sites you've visited—often long after you've either purchased the product you searched for or perhaps lost interest all together. Retargeting is a highly effective technique that employs cookies to enable marketers to remain top of mind with prospects after initial interest is shown. Retargeting can also occur cross-platform as services like Rentrak capture viewing data, then share it with mobile ad networks to follow the consumer from the television screen to the mobile device. It's an efficient way of reinforcing the television commercial through added frequency on other platforms to increase top of mind awareness and drive ROI.

COMPARING TRADITIONAL & ONLINE MEDIA TRANSACTIONS

Traditional media, with the exception of exclusive premium television content, is relegated to competing on a lower cost per thousand rate than their digital media counterparts due to their inability to identify and target a message to an individual consumer. Broadcasters, cable nets and MVPDs are working with vendors like Rentrak to use the set-top box as a means of serving addressable ads to households. It improves upon the one-to-many "broadcast" model of television and cable programming to help leverage large audiences for network programming with more customized ad solutions. As television invariably shifts to IP distribution through various OTT services including products offered by incumbent MVPDs (cable and satellite providers), the ability to become part of the digital ad ecosystem will vastly improve, though it's not guaranteed that ad rates and yield will grow due to the ever-increasing supply of premium online video inventory.

Compared to the traditional or legacy media transaction, purchasing impressions online can be much faster even though it is infinitely more complex. This sounds paradoxical, but is essentially the product of workflow automation where machines, if properly programmed, have the ability to make faster and better decisions than people performing the same task. The agency planner and buyer along with the media seller are now being aided or replaced by sophisticated algorithms which identify available impressions from thousands of publishers, build target audiences to fit the client's objectives and then secure the highest quality impressions at the most efficient cost to drive sales lift for the client. The increased complexity is due to the layers of "middlemen" who co-exist in the value chain between the marketer and the publisher.

The 4 C's will very much apply to ad buying—both digital and traditional—as marketers opt for value, speed and automation through connectivity, convenience, choice and cost to drive their marketing ROI. The legacy high-touch process of traditional media buying is simply anathema to the new Modern Media ecosystem. Input and decisions around strategy and planning will continue to be driven by key personnel on both the buy and sell side, but the execution function will largely be automated in the years ahead.

AD TECH DRIVES THE VALUE PROPOSITION OF DIGITAL MARKETING

Data Management Platforms (DMPs) are the cloud-based data warehouses that tie all of the various data sets together to create distinct audience segments. These custom segments can then be targeted by marketers through online ads reaching individual users who match a particular profile. DMPs are used by agencies, marketers and publishers alike. Agencies covet the data and analyze it across individual client campaigns as well as cross-client to gain insights on audience segments, engagement and activation or conversion. DMPs are becoming essential tools to help marketers plan and execute more personalized campaigns across digital media channels by providing the necessary information to plan and optimize the media buy for both buy- and sell-side.

Demand Side Platforms serve as buy-side aggregators working with a vast array of agencies and marketers to help them buy impressions and execute campaigns across a range of publisher sites. They have developed tools that enable advertisers to manage complex targeting parameters across several different ad exchanges with a central user interface. DSPs also facilitate programmatic ad buying through real-time bidding also known as RTB. Many publishers are concerned about commoditizing their prime inventory, however, which is an impediment to widespread adoption of real-time bidding. Consequently, DSPs can also buy premium inventory at fixed prices, rather than bid in an auction, if the premium inventory they're looking for isn't offered through an exchange in real time.

Supply Side Platforms serve to mirror many of the same functions for publishers that DSPs provide for advertisers. SSPs work with individual publishers to maximize the value of their inventory by helping them package and present their inventory in the most advantageous way to the demand side (advertisers). SSPs allow publishers to set price floors and control which inventory is brought to market versus what premium inventory is reserved for the publisher's direct sales team to be sold directly to key clients or reserved for a higher yield than offered through a programmatic channel. SSPs business intelligence tools also help publishers gauge market demand for their content, which in turn helps them iterate their content mix to improve overall yield in addition to aggregating multiple exchanges to maximize the available pool of buyers.

AD EXCHANGES & PROGRAMMATIC

Exchanges are digital marketplaces where impressions are bought and sold like stocks, bonds or commodities. DSPs engage in real-time bidding through multiple ad exchanges as publishers working through SSPs are also presenting inventory on various exchanges on the supply side. Unlike the stock market where you would place a buy order in for a specific security, a great deal of the inventory for sale on exchanges is done so anonymously because publishers seek to protect their direct sales channel for key clients where they command premium rates. Publishers tend to rely on exchanges for remnant inventory that they "tip" into various exchanges anonymously through SSPs. Most exchanges are open, but a number of publishers employ private exchanges that are not open to DSPs or SSPs. They are only available to marketers by invitation and are used to control pricing for premium inventory and give preferred clients an automated workflow process for efficiency, but full transparency with respect to the publisher's impressions. Private exchanges will be increasingly adopted by traditional media companies as they automate their sales functions to manage costs and respond to the demand from their clients and agency partners.

Publisher's restrictions aside, programmatic is the fastest growing segment in advertising. It's driven essentially by real-time auctions conducted primarily over open (non-private) exchanges. As the digital advertising ecosystem continues to evolve, marketers are shifting more ad spend to digital and more of their digital spend to programmatic due to its efficiency. The quality of data and analytics continue to improve and the time spent with digital media continues to increase thus creating ever more available impressions to bid for. Programmatic is becoming the preferred method for advertising transactions and will eventually account for the majority of spend much the same way as online bookings now account for the majority of travel expenditures.

Over time, agencies and media companies will evolve the structure of their respective organizations to reflect the shift away from legacy negotiations between buyers and sellers to an organization capable of executing direct and RTB programmatic ad sales at scale. The legacy structure has been the standard practice for decades with very little innovation to streamline the process as both media companies and agencies are staffed to execute transactions against a highly personnel-intensive workflow. Programmatic will help advertisers plan campaigns more optimally through audience measurement and customer insights as the ad buy becomes more about the context of an individual impression including identify and intent, and less about the specific piece of content in which the impression is made.

From the advertiser's perspective, however, there are some advantages to the legacy systems due to relatively low friction costs paid to the agency to plan, negotiate and execute the buy. Contrast this model to digital media where viable publishers number in the thousands, not dozens like traditional media. Except for the largest publishers like Google, Facebook and Verizon's AOL and Yahoo, the long tail of digital content publishers are not going to have access to CMOs or agency planners to pitch their product. Ad networks were originally developed to aggregate publishers across the web and bring their inventory to market and the digital ad market evolved out of this structure. Ad networks were followed by exchanges and now it has evolved in to the current structure of DMPs, SSPs and DSPs transacting through low-margin exchanges. Compared to the legacy analog structure, the cost to move a dollar from the marketer to the publisher is too high which will lead to more end-to-end solutions by large ad tech players like Google and Facebook and others. As transparency improves and the inevitable value chain consolidation occurs, transaction costs will be reduced, fueling a continued shift to digital and more ad spend transacted programmatically.

TECHNOLOGY DRIVES THE CREATIVE PROCESS

The technology used to optimize targeting and determine the value of a given impression in milliseconds is also being employed to iterate on optimizing the creative message. The nirvana of marketing is to serve the right message to the right target prospect at the right time at the right price. Sounds simple, but it has been an ever-elusive goal that has been the bane of the marketers, prompting the preamble that "half my ad dollars are wasted, but I don't know which half." To maximize ROI for the marketer, it's imperative to not only hit the target at the right moment, but to do so with the optimal message while buying the impressions at the lowest possible price.

In a message-saturated environment, only the most effective creative truly resonates with the target consumer, causing them to engage them with the brand. This is the first step towards activation or purchase with the goal of building a relationship with the consumer that ultimately leads to repurchase and brand advocacy to new target prospects. America is no longer the homogeneous society of the Mad Men era and thus the creative challenge is infinitely more complex. Market segmentation through behavioral data—both empirical and modeled—requires a more nuanced creative blueprint developed through frequent iteration. The real-time feedback of consumers choosing to engage with an ad—or not—is beneficial to marketers who no longer have to make big creative bets on mass targeted media with a "spray and pray" strategy. Digital technology enables marketers to begin the creative process with a fundamentally better understanding of their target consumer including numerous heterogeneous segments that are best addressed with slightly different messages. Sophisticated analytics testing enable marketers to analyze complex data sets of consumers, creative and context to optimize a campaign.

Consequently, multiple creative treatments can be developed which are then tested in real time to improve the potential for successful consumer en-

gagement. In the data-driven creative process, the last mile is the ability to select the optimal creative for the target consumer in real time considering the
context of time, location and device. Technology will not be the gating issue in
this process, but rather it will be the speed at which marketers evolve their organizations including both people and process to take advantage of sophisticated
data analytics. Netflix and Amazon are both data-driven organizations that are
both employing data science in their respective content strategies. From crowd-
sourced submissions to iterative content testing and empirical data on viewing
habits, the digital video distributors are fine-tuning their content strategies to
drive subscriber growth and reduce churn.

Another important tool for marketers afforded by digital technology is the
ability to develop interactive messaging with target consumers. The original
and most rudimentary form of interactive digital ads have been click-through
ads. A consumer likes what they see in an ad and clicks to buy or get more
information. Interactive pay per click ads have been prominent in the growth
of search and display advertising, and now interactive ads for brand advertising are becoming an exciting area for investment by marketers. Brands want
to build relationships with their consumers, which require a richer, more engaged communication strategy to complement or replace an industry standard
30-second commercial announcement. Commercials still have an important
role to play in driving awareness and stimulating demand at the top of the marketing funnel, but brands increasingly want to engage with their consumers on
a more personal level to build a more meaningful relationship. Brands, like the
people who buy them, have a story, which needs to be told. Interactive ads are
another new dimension for marketers, enabled by technology, to engage and
activate target consumers. The most successful ad campaigns will adhere to the
same fundamentals of the most successful media brands—they will be multiplatform integrations with a consistent brand ethos. Disney and Apple serve as
exemplars of this brand marketing discipline.

PRIVACY CONCERNS & AD BLOCKING

Beginning with the Snowden-NSA scandal, public awareness of privacy and data sharing has been heightened. It's balanced by people's belief that government surveillance is an essential weapon in combating terrorism, and secondly, by people's increasing demand for a personalized online experience including content, advertising and commerce. Privacy policies including data collection and sharing are disclosed by law for websites which collect personal data, but the fine print is rarely read and consumers simply click "Agree" and get on with their business. Information sharing is therefore not a likely threat to online data collection, but ad-blocking software could be disruptive to the online advertising ecosystem. If consumers find mobile, display or video ads to be a nuisance, they can install software or download apps, which will block browser ads and potentially in-app ads on mobile if not "approved" by the ad blocking software. For obvious reasons, this would upset the free content, ad-supported model that dominates the online experience. Moreover, two of the three key protagonists—Facebook, Google and Apple—have a vested interest in preserving the current model because they earn most all of their revenue from advertising. Apple, however, has divergent interests from Facebook and Google as their business model relies on device sales and if they can make their user experience more desirable by eliminating perceived clutter, they will sell more devices. Publishers could react to lost revenue by erecting paywalls or altering the user experience for consumers who employ ad-blocking software on their devices, which would serve as a strong disincentive to the widespread adoption of ad-blocking technology. The competing objectives of the key constituencies will play out over time, but consumers appear to be less concerned about privacy than they are with a convenient user experience that is often free of charge.

ADVERTISING WILL BECOME MORE TARGETED AND LESS EXPENSIVE

The rapid growth of consumer's time spent with digital media combined with the advances in data-driven ad technology are having a profound impact on media and advertising. More digital content is being consumed than ever before which is generating more available ad impressions than ever before. Technology is progressing rapidly to enable marketers to access virtually all available inventory on a per impression basis. The vast amounts of user data (core and derivative) combined with the ability to serve ads directly to individual users create smarter impressions that are increasingly being bought and placed through programmatic or automated workflow processes. Rapidly growing supply and rapidly improving access to that supply are outstripping demand with the changes upending legacy business models and organizational structures. Innovations in data management, ad tech, automated and programmatic ad buying with real-time bidding along with dynamic ad serving are conspiring to make advertising cheaper, smarter, real time and highly accountable. It's evolving quickly and must work through the negatives of having too many disparate components creating high friction costs as well as the ongoing challenges with fraud and lack of transparency.

Long term, the competitive market place will sort out these issues including likely consolidation of the digital marketing value chain with the expected outcome driving greater simplicity, efficiency and transparency. Simply put, both traditional and online media companies are growing available impressions at a faster rate than either consumer spending or the attendant ad markets are growing. The result is ongoing pricing pressure on the value of an impression, which is being intensified by the ability to transact more efficiently due to data-driven targeting technology. The need to engage target consumers from the top of the funnel (awareness) to the bottom of the funnel (purchase) remains constant, but the market is and will continue to become more efficient and transparent with ad dollars continuing to shift to digital as new and traditional media ecosystems come together in the era of Modern Media.

10 | THE BUNDLE SLIMS DOWN TO SURVIVE: PRESSURE ON THE PAY TV ECOSYSTEM

Much has been written about the disaggregation of the pay TV bundle with analysts intently focused on the quarterly losses of video subscribers by the large distributors or MVPDs (multichannel video program distributors). At its peak in 2012, the combined total of U.S. pay television subscribers to cable, satellite and telco services was approximately 103 million. That number is expected to continue to decline over time as consumers opt for more efficient and bespoke subscription offerings as substitutes for the traditional 180+ channel bundle. The alternatives are growing rapidly and include smaller or "skinny" bundles from existing legacy providers in addition to offerings from the OTT or over-the-top distributors like Apple, Amazon, Netflix, Hulu, Sony and others.

According to Nielsen's Advertising & Audiences Report, the average U.S. TV home now receives 189 TV channels—a record high and significant jump since 2008, when the average home received 129 channels. Despite this increase, consumers have consistently tuned in to an average of just 17 channels on a weekly basis. Consumers are paying for a full bundle and watching less than 10 percent of it, which presents an opportunity for a more efficient consumer offering. Over time, OTT entrants like Hulu, Sony, Apple TV and Sling TV will emerge and existing distributors will disrupt themselves with alternative offerings giving the consumer more perceived value and flexibility.

The TV Bundle itself is being slowly replaced by smaller, custom packages and DTC à la carte offerings. DTC (direct to consumer) offerings were non-existent a few years ago, but they are beginning to gain some traction as media companies hedge their bets on cord-cutting by going direct to their viewers through subscription-based apps. HBO, Showtime and CBS are among early entrants with successful DTC offerings. For broadcast networks, going direct to consumer is a smart hedge against cord-cutting, but it's even a smarter negotiation ploy against local broadcasters for a greater share of the retransmission fees paid by the distributors, which are expected to reach $10 billion by 2020.

The bundle will naturally be slow to unravel because inertia is a very powerful force and two out of three stakeholders have a vested interest in maintaining the status quo. Both the content providers and the video distributors enjoy a very profitable industry and have no incentive to accelerate the disaggregation of the bundle. Most consumers still perceive their pay TV and broadband package to be a reasonable value in spite of watching just 10 percent of available channels. Existing carriage agreements also prevent the MVPDs from dropping channels and likewise, prevent some channels from launching DTC apps. Cord-cutting makes for a juicy story in the press, but the rate of decline of pay TV subscriptions would have to increase dramatically from the current rate of less than 1 percent per year to have a material impact on the core pay TV ecosystem in the near term. Marginally rated channels, however, will be among the first to feel the pain when their carriage agreements come up for renewal.

The bundle also includes high-speed broadband, which has become increasingly more important to consumers who are watching ever more bandwidth intensive online video. Cable companies in most markets have the leverage to raise broadband prices when purchased as a stand-alone service to serve as a powerful disincentive to cut the cord in favor of an OTT offering. Consumers will likely view the marginal utility of the content—given the broadband-only price—as both attractive and convenient. There simply aren't enough broadband alternatives to create a truly efficient marketplace where consumers can efficiently price content and broadband separately. Mobile offers a potential OTT alternative to cable, but at present, it's not sufficiently robust to meet the bandwidth intensive needs of 1080p video let alone the emerging 4K, 8K and even VR technologies.

The MVPDs (distributors) are responding to consumer demands for mobile access to the content they are paying for. Coined by Time Warner Chief Jeff Bewkes as "TV Everywhere," the concept is premised that paying customers should be able to access all of the content they receive by cable or satellite on mobile devices or PCs through digital streaming delivered over wireless or wireline broadband. Users simply "authenticate" their pay subscription to the content app and they are permissioned to receive the digital video stream of selected content. This option only serves to enhance the value proposition of the bundle to the consumer, giving them the best of both worlds and allowing them to enjoy their favorite content wherever they are. Continuity and incremental use cases will serve to preserve the status quo of the pay TV ecosystem for the foreseeable future, but the total number of subscribers for the full 180+ channel bundle will continue to decline.

NO CRASH DIETS

The "bundle" won't go away, but it will evolve over time depending upon the options offered by legacy video distributors as well as the new competitive offerings from OTT entrants like Netflix, Amazon and Hulu. Expect a host of new video on demand (VOD) offerings whether ad-supported (AVOD) or subscription-based (SVOD) to emerge in the coming years. Current market leaders, Netflix, Amazon and Hulu will see increased competition from tech giants like Apple, Google, Facebook, Sony and Microsoft. Pay TV distributors will also offer alternatives as evidenced by Dish's Sling TV as well as other similar OTT services are expected to be offered by cable companies.

Lastly, the programmers themselves are going direct to consumers with individual channel subscriptions or by bundling assets within their respective stables to create content packages that consumers will find appealing. Invariably, there will be a period of intense experimentation of pricing and packages to find points of inflection where various consumer segments will find value and transact. It will take years to educate consumers broadly on new technology and the options it now creates which in turn will make marketing prowess a potential source of competitive advantage. The wireless industry is experiencing the same phenomenon as it expands service offerings to meet consumer demand for mobile data and remains heavily promotional.

Smaller, more bespoke offerings will slowly gain traction as Millennials increasingly form households and become pay TV customers. This important demographic cohort's behavior has been exhorted as the future of video because they don't watch linear television, but rather, they consume on-demand video and don't delineate between traditional channels and digital apps. It's all content and Millennials want to program and control their own experience and they are just as content to view it on a tablet or phone as they are on a television set. This narrative is provocative and makes for good copy, but in reality, society is not that permanently bifurcated. In other words, Millennials assimilate over time much the same way that the Gen X and Gen Y generations have done. On a historical basis, Millennials are a few years late in household formation—mostly due to the lingering effects of the Great Recession—but once they make the fundamental change to form a household, their inevitable assimilation drives consumption patterns much closer to societal norms but culturally, they will be much more open to new solutions and less beholden to conventional practices than previous generations.

In addition to choice, the new smaller bundles can also offer a better user experience which consumers may regard as a superior value proposition. Sony Vue on PlayStation is a good example of a desirable user experience with a skinny bundle on an SVOD platform. Apple has been trying to "crack the code" on television for years and now appears to have innovated their television product to support a content-centric strategy where iPhones, iPads, Macs and TVs are all connected screens rather than individual mediums. Pay TV distributors are also intent upon improving the user experience. They are innovating their user interface to provide a more contemporary entertainment experience designed to reduce the higher churn rates they experience from Millennials. For example, some MVPDs have permitted subscribers to substitute a Roku box for their cable box and now the FCC has mandated that consumers may replace their leased cable boxes with third-party offerings. Roku's progressive interface allows subscribers to easily switch between linear pay TV offerings and OTT content by Netflix, Amazon Prime and host of others. This seamless experience for the user will undoubtedly increase in importance as the OTT platforms gain widespread adoption driven by the massive investments in content and marketing that the largest platforms are currently making.

The new SVOD offerings, including Netflix, Amazon, Hulu, and Apple TV will continue to serve primarily as incremental video services rather than substitutes for existing Pay TV bundles. Of Netflix's over 40 million domestic subscribers, approximately two-thirds are also subscribing to Pay TV. It looks as though a skinnier bundle giving consumers more choice on what's included in their video package, coupled with one or more OTT services could be a popular alternative for the majority of current Pay TV subscribers.

The OTT platforms with designs on taking share from the exiting cable bundle include: Netflix, Apple TV, Hulu, Roku, TiVo, YouTube, Amazon, Sony and several others. For the reasons discussed in this chapter, it's more likely that they will continue to complement rather than cannibalize the existing bundle. As these new entrants continue to innovate the user experience, so too will the Pay TV distributors or MVPDs. The consumer will once again be the big winner across each of the 4 C's—connectivity, convenience, choice and cost. In short, OTT platforms will initially serve to complement traditional pay TV offerings rather than replace them. Developers will innovate the user interfaces and your iPhone or Android screen will extend to your television set and car dashboard—just a different sized screen. Channels will be replaced by apps that are à la carte or aggregated in skinny bundles and will increasingly be interactive to help customize the viewing experience and even provide ecommerce and service-type opportunities. It's the path to personalized TV and ultimately to a completely personalized media experience, and it will be executed through a mobile operating system because the app experience is preferable and more intuitive to consumers and importantly, it provides a way for consumers to transact directly with the content provider.

What will change, however, is the fundamental concept of a linear channel. Over the next decade, as channels give way to sophisticated apps that offer the linear channel as well as all of its discrete programming elements on demand and much more including interactive features and commerce. In addition, depending upon the channel or network, the direct to consumer app could offer additional content such as short-form videos, games, audio and books. A good example of this new model is Disney Life, which was recently launched in Europe. Multimedia digital apps like Disney Life can offer a more compelling user experience than linear television alone. Movies, television, music, magazines and books can all live in a branded app that offers a more engaging user experience than a linear television channel. The multiplatform brand model will be packaged nicely on an app that is optimized for each device and can present a compelling value proposition as a standalone DTC subscription service or bundled with a complementary basket of channels.

Ultimately, it will depend upon the array of competitive offerings including DTC apps, OTT platforms, and inexpensive channel bundles that will determine how far and how fast the changes to the current Pay TV ecosystem will occur. The key for content owners and distributors will be effective market segmentation to determine price elasticity and identify content demands. Lastly, the smaller bundles also known as "skinny bundles" will be in greater demand by consumers interested in maximizing value for their entertainment dollar.

The current pay television ecosystem is clearly subsidizing more than a few dozen channels that remain on consumer's channel guides and contribute to their monthly bill when the ratings indicate that most consumers have little interest in watching them. Customized offerings like AppleTV and Sling TV are the first real threat to the 180+ channel bundle, but the key takeaway is that it will take several years to materially disrupt the current ecosystem.

Moreover, programmers will feel the pinch before distributors because distributors have alternate revenue streams which they can price accordingly to defend their business model including standalone broadband, voice and home security whereas programmers have just two revenue streams—sub fees and advertising—and both are adversely affected by a declining sub base, not to mention the lack of leverage in carriage renewal negotiations.

11 | ON DEMAND IS IN DEMAND

"On demand" has become firmly ingrained in the lexicon of the digital economy and serves as the key point of differentiation between linear and nonlinear media. The ability to call or access specific pieces of content at any time has been liberating for consumers, causing a sea change in their media consumption behavior. Over time, consumers are being conditioned to disaggregate analog content providers like television channels and newspapers in favor of the fundamental units of content they distribute. In their traditional form, these "aggregators" of content no longer present the optimal use case to consumers who prefer a more personalized experience serving their favorite shows rather than traditional linear channels on television. Similarly, a growing number of consumers now prefer to read select articles of interest served conveniently in a newsfeed as opposed to searching through entire newspapers for content.

Take, for example, a copy of the New York Times and think about it as a series of stories ranging from headlines, international news, domestic news, local New York news, business news, sports, culture, entertainment and opinion. It's an enormous amount of content delivered in a "one size fits all" format by necessity to serve a diverse audience. The first iteration of print moving to digital was simply a replica of the physical copy online. This quickly evolved due to the ability to search and sort in order to help make the experience more user-friendly and personalized. Features such as push content were also added to create an "alerts" product for notifications. This on-demand content experience was increasingly individualized, but still very much associated with the brand of the New York Times. This is true for most newspapers and magazines as they've evolved their digital presence.

What began with third-party aggregators like Huffington Post (who initially drove traffic by cleverly rewriting the headlines of digital publishers to capture search traffic and serve ads while linking to the original content) has transitioned to more brand agnostic content being woven into newsfeeds of popular social networks and messaging apps. News and information content can vary widely from Pulitzer Prize winning journalism to your neighbor writing a review on a local restaurant. The playing field for distribution and consumer utility for these two examples of digital content is more level than ever before and driven by user preferences as opposed to the cultural arbiters who have long shaped the content offering of linear media.

The "bundle" of branded content found in newspapers, newscasts and magazines is now being challenged by consumer's desire to program their own content experience for news and information. More than half the population (and growing) now relies on social apps and messaging networks for their news and information. The strategy of news content providers to push downloads of their proprietary apps in order to create a walled-garden content experience appears to be at odds with the way people want to consume news and information. They are instead, opting for a constantly connected solution that is convenient to use, offers abundant choice and all at no cost. Sound familiar?

Facebook Instant Articles represents yet another important step function in the disaggregation and dilution of branded content channels. Users indicate preferences both explicitly and implicitly through their conversations, searches and postings. Content can be pushed to them through their newsfeeds directly without the inconvenient user-experience of having to link to a website and wait for the content to load. The feature essentially aggregates all of the relevant content from a vast array of participating publishers for each individual user and serves it to them in their newsfeed. According to Pew, over one-third of Americans are now using Facebook as their primary news source. The value proposition is clear for the users as they're now able to conveniently receive a custom briefing on the topics they find useful and important. This number will rise as more premium content is availed to the site and served with a personalized and seamless user experience.

This may prove to be a Faustian bargain for publishers, however, as the cost per digital impression declines due to ever-increasing supply of inventory and the need for greater traffic and ever more page views intensifies. Facebook represents an ocean of potential traffic for publishers they would otherwise not be exposed to, but the new users, however, are reading individual stories that are detached from the publisher's brand. Moreover, the traffic stays on Facebook as the need to link to the publisher's site has largely been eliminated. Publishers have the option to sell the ad inventory themselves, but as scale and rich data become the two most important attributes for competing in an increasingly automated ad market, selling against Facebook's sophisticated monetization machine will likely yield sub-optimal results leading publishers to elect to have Facebook sell the ads for a negotiated selling concession.

Facebook as well as Instagram, YouTube and Twitter have historically produced almost no content, yet they are capturing a significant share of the advertising market. They mostly rely on user generated content or third-party publishers to drive traffic, which is then offered to marketers as "smart impressions" through the capture, and manipulation of the user's own data. Publishers made the early mistake of allowing search engines and third-party aggregators access to their content, which they in turn used to build audiences on the backs of the content publishers. It was a blatant value transfer from the publisher to the clever distributers who repackaged the publisher's content on their own branded site—all made possible through the new digital distribution channel.

It was a miscalculation by publishers that "freemium" traffic and page views were a healthy sampling mechanism to expose more users to their digital content with the hopes that a subscription would soon follow. The unintended consequence was a change in consumer's perception of value for journalistic content. Most people used to regularly pay for newspapers and recorded music, but now both are widely available for no cost. The net effect has reduced the conversion rates of "freemium" models to a fraction of what publishers, labels and streaming services originally modeled. Similar to print journalism, the music industry has also witnessed a decline in perceived value of their product, but mostly because of piracy and the availability of individual songs as opposed to being forced to buy the album in order to get the song. Consumers have been exposed to a myriad of options to access free content and have been conditioned to believe that most news and information content should be both on demand and free of charge. This has caused publishers to become more reliant on digital ad revenue and has intensified pressure on publishers to find more traffic and marketable impressions, but tasked to do so with fewer marketing resources.

Expect Facebook Instant Articles and other similar types of customized aggregations on scaled platforms to gain traction as publishers are forced to chase traffic and revenue in the short run to support the high fixed costs of producing content. As more news is consumed away from the physical or digital "walled garden" of the branded content producers, the less relevant the brands ultimately become. Particularly in journalism, look for the perceived value over time to transfer to the digital distribution platforms as well as the content creators themselves and away from the umbrella brand of the media company. For example, if you follow a sports team, the veteran local beat writer's individual brand and the content they serve through Facebook or Twitter newsfeeds may have more value to fans than the media company employing the beat writer. As this shift continues to gain momentum, the sports journalist may realize that he could go it alone and make more money by having

Facebook and others monetize his work directly and he may also partner with local radio and television to create additional branded content over multiple platforms. This will exacerbate the decline of traffic to the branded newspaper site as the fundamental producers of content leave the mother ship creating a vicious cycle that could accelerate the demise of the brand.

ON DEMAND DRIVES THE SHARING ECONOMY

In addition to the structural changes it's causing in media, on demand is also the underpinning of what is known as the "sharing economy." At the root of this new paradigm is consumer's preference for access, rather than ownership of either physical or virtual goods. Consumers and businesses don't need to own certain assets if they can simply pay as they go and only for what they use. Early, non-digital examples of this would be fractional ownership of aircraft, boats, vacation homes, fine jewelry and office space. This "pooled-asset" concept enabled consumers to enjoy all of an asset part of the time, promising efficiency and convenience. Fractional ownership has become a large and growing industry and has served as the model for the digital applications promoting and enabling the sharing economy.

Uber and Airbnb have become significant players in the sharing economy by offering consumers access to an existing asset base of cars and rooms which were previously unconnected and not in service. In the case of Uber, they have over 200,000 drivers in the U.S. alone that is roughly equal to the number of taxis in the country. An app has roughly doubled the available car-service inventory in a highly regulated industry virtually overnight, which is illustrative of the power and potential of the sharing economy. More people now have convenient access to transportation and cars are being used more efficiently which should have positive implications on productivity in addition to greater societal benefits like fewer drunk drivers on the road and flexible job creation.

Another outstanding, digital distribution success is Airbnb which is to lodging what Uber is to ground transportation. It now claims to offer access to over two million rooms for rent, which is more than the total inventory of Marriott, Hilton and Hyatt hotels combined. Similar to Uber, it has tapped into a supply of potential inventory, which can be "activated" into a marketplace. The benefits to society are greater competition which drives price and choice for consumers. For homeowners, it creates an opportunity to monetize their largest asset, potentially raising their standard of living. The sharing economy will continue to expand where underutilized assets can efficiently be organized and brought to market with a consumer value proposition based upon the 4 C's and the best business models will be competitively insulated by the network effect similar to the competitive protections enjoyed by first-movers Uber and Airbnb.

CLOUD EFFECTS

The "cloud" is probably the most liberally used, yet least understood term in modern technology. For starters, the "cloud" is not some amorphous, ether-based stream of data floating over the airwaves, but rather a series of giant, secure, heavily air-conditioned rooms full of servers which process and store digital data. There are several different clouds, both private and public, and they don't necessarily communicate with one another. Amazon has built a market-leading business, Amazon Web Services (AWS), by selling computing power and storage based upon the number of users of a specific application and the amount of bandwidth and storage they collectively consume. Because they are renting capacity, enterprises can scale up or down depending upon growth rates or seasonality without having to purchase and maintain the hardware. Facebook has an enormous investment in a private cloud, which stores and processes its user and advertiser data across its many sites and apps. Google and Microsoft have built their own private clouds, but also sell cloud-computing services to the public as the enterprise shift to the cloud along with "big data" analytics have become the two most important trends in information technology.

Large players increasingly dominate cloud computing led by Amazon's AWS and include Google, Microsoft, Facebook, IBM, HP, AT&T and Verizon. These large cloud providers along with thousands of smaller players in over 3 million data centers account for almost 10 percent of the nation's electricity use and this figure is growing as more applications and devices come online. Tech giants' product and brand advertising is replete with references to the "cloud" which promises to revolutionize the way we use software and storage. The "cloud" metaphor—though not descriptive of the large server farms it refers to—is a useful way to describe the computing workflow which processes and stores information that can be received from or transmitted to any connected device with an IP address. The ability to access and control devices via the internet is aggressively driving the next wave of connectivity known as the "Internet of Things" or IoT and will have profound implications on the future of media as it enables content creators and distributors to create an intelligent and highly personalized, cross-platform experience.

The way the cloud works is fairly straightforward. Applications and data are stored on the cloud's servers, which are then activated when connected devices such as smartphones or PCs send queries and data to specific applications in the cloud for processing and storage. The cloud servers then process them as instructed and return the data or answers back to the device through the app. For example, when you book a flight through an airline app, your phone is communicating with the airline's app or website including its database of customer information, current inventory and pricing. It enables you to find a flight, book it, select a seat and pay for it in just a couple of minutes from your smartphone or PC. Your device is not processing the data, it merely enables two-way accesses to the cloud which in turn contains the applications, processing power and data necessary to execute the transaction.

Prior to introduction of the "cloud," a seminal shift in the business model for enterprise software companies from ownership to access took root and served as a harbinger for the on demand, as well as the sharing economy business models. Software as a Service or "SaaS" was first introduced around the time the Web 2.0 movement was gaining traction following the dotcom bust in 2001. The SaaS model of on-demand computing quickly gained popularity with enterprise customers because it offered several important advantages over the legacy ownership model, but not necessarily for the vendors themselves. Consequently, the rapid adoption of the SaaS model disrupted the enterprise computing market for hardware, software and storage compelling traditional software publishers and hardware vendors to make wholesale changes to their competitive strategies or risk irrelevance—similar to the disruption facing the traditional media ecosystem. Enterprise software has historically been sold to customers requiring a cash outlay up front for hardware and software, as well as a dedicated staff to host and maintain the applications. It's very expensive and labor intensive to customize, install and maintain hardware and software solutions for the enterprise. The SaaS model quickly gained popularity with business customers because it offered a "plug and play" alternative that lead to increased productivity and greater efficiencies. The SaaS model is another example of an innovative new—and highly disruptive—business model for computing that delivers on the value proposition of the 4 C's—connectivity, convenience, choice and cost.

SaaS applications are also beneficiaries of the network effect where a diverse user group provides feedback to improve the application, which in turn benefits all of the users in real time who license the product. The SaaS model enables enterprises to efficiently rent rather than buy software, thus avoiding long term commitments and maintaining flexibility to switch products or even vendors with minimal friction costs. The SaaS model has exploded with the advent of centralized cloud computing which enables users to access software or storage via the internet rather than incurring the heavy expense to locally host and maintain the applications and data storage. The "cloud" has created an on-demand distribution channel for software just as it has for media and commerce.

Salesforce was an early advocate of the new distribution channel of cloud computing in launching a CRM application, then quickly evolving and expanding their business through a series of acquisitions to embrace a fundamental shift to the cloud distribution channel for all software and storage. As cloud evangelists, Salesforce has led a fundamental shift in thinking which has now achieved critical mass, touting the benefits of cloud computing as enabling businesses and consumers to use and pay only for what they need and only when they need it. Enterprise software, which includes everything from sales orders, inventory management, finance, accounting, HR, benefits, CRM, procurement and facilities, has historically been hosted on site and maintained by the user, but a more efficient "cloud-based" model has the application and storage live in the cloud where it is accessed by the end user for a subscription fee. Unlike a physical asset such as an airplane, which can only fly one mission at a time, software is a virtual, digital asset, which can run across a fully distributed network of users making it an even stronger candidate for the "sharing" model, which also holds true for digital media content.

Today, virtually all software publishers are focused on cloud-based solutions for both the enterprise and consumer markets. Amazon, Microsoft, and Google are all aggressively investing in large data centers and infrastructure to host cloud-based software applications and the attendant need for data storage. The massive investment required to compete will limit the number of entrants, but the resulting product offerings and price points will help stimulate innovation and create lower barriers to entry by reducing capital-intensive tech build-outs for start-ups.

THE CLOUD ENABLES ON DEMAND MEDIA

The "cloud" has become the ideal distribution technology for nonlinear media content because of its accessibility. Content providers can easily upload virtually limitless pieces of content, which are then stored and accessed on demand by users through any connected device. YouTube is an excellent example of cloud-based, nonlinear digital content distribution. Producers upload their content into the cloud and YouTube enables users to search and discover content, which is then streamed from the cloud for viewing. It's a terrific service for both producers and users who both can access it for free. YouTube derives most of its revenue from video advertising "pre-roll" which are short commercial announcements prior to the start of a video. It's more than a $5 billion business and is expected to surpass each of the four broadcast networks (ABC, CBS, FOX and NBC) in ad revenue within a few years. It's another poignant illustration of the democratization of media content and the value shift to scaled digital distributors. Through the acquisition of YouTube, Google has created a substantial media business without producing any content, but rather making it easy and affordable for producers to connect with consumers while building a very successful digital distribution media business with high entry barriers due to the network effect.

On-demand content is expanding rapidly into television, music, games, newspapers, magazines, books and e-learning. Media is a perfect candidate for an on-demand model because of the nature of its product. Content can be housed in virtual "libraries" and served simultaneously to an unlimited base of users across numerous devices in virtually any location. A number of on-demand video (VOD) "channels" are forming to meet exploding consumer demand for nonlinear video content streamed to connected devices. The most popular on-demand video service is Netflix, which is known as an SVOD or Subscription Video On Demand service. HBO GO, Amazon and Apple TV are all SVOD services along with competitors, Hulu and YouTube, which both began as AVOD or ad-supported video on demand and subsequently added a premium subscription offering without ads.

Netflix is the world's most valuable SVOD business, but employs a very different strategy from YouTube, which is the world's most valuable AVOD business. Whereas YouTube's content is almost entirely user-generated, Netflix spends over $5 billion a year on a mix of original content ranging from television series and movies to reruns from broadcast and cable networks, as well as major studios to license windows to air first-run motion pictures and library content. Netflix is in a pitched battle with HBO, Showtime and Amazon to dominate the premium video on demand space. Amazon is also an aggressive new entrant with content ambitions to compete successfully through its SVOD offering called Amazon Prime Instant Video. Amazon is spending over $2 billion per year on content and that figure is expected to grow rapidly as competition for SVOD customers intensifies.

YouTube has also moved beyond its AVOD roots to introduce YouTube Red as monthly subscription or SVOD service without ads. They plan to license television shows, movies and produce original content with some of existing YouTube platform stars because it's unlikely that an ad-free subscription service without a slate of exclusive, premium content will be enough of a draw to build a sustainable subscriber base. It's not clear how many over-the-top (OTT) subscription video services an individual consumer will opt to pay for, but it's clear that that consumers will have to make choices between a number of services as they construct their own personal bundle between pay television and OTT options.

As the competition between distributors for the best content intensifies, the cost of producing premium quality television is rising as broadcast networks along with HBO, Netflix, Amazon, Showtime, Turner and Hulu all compete for writers, producers, scripts and actors. The rate of investment into television content has risen dramatically as traditional networks feel the competitive pressure of the SVOD's commitment to content and is driving what the industry is calling "The Golden Age of Television."

On-demand content will continue gaining popularity because it offers a superior user experience in both choice and convenience than consumers have historically enjoyed with linear television. With on demand, the consumer is in control of what, when and where they consume the content as opposed to a linear model where content is "pushed" at the user and sequenced in a rigid format giving the consumer no real-time alternatives except to use a DVR. In the linear model, television networks also counter-program one another and build schedules to maximize audience flow to drive sampling and ratings for new shows. For the user, this type of content experience is a more passive than purposeful viewing experience. Conversely, you don't watch Netflix as a linear network, but rather, you watch programs in its library on any of the four screens (TV, PC, tablet or smartphone) at any time you choose. Netflix knows exactly how many streams it serves, but like Amazon, never discusses audience or ratings because their respective business models are not ad-dependent and they want to use their proprietary data to inform future production decisions. Unlike linear television where you must conform to the content provider's schedule, the only appointment viewing in an on-demand environment is with yourself, your friends and family. Netflix, Amazon Prime Instant Video, Hulu, Apple TV, CBS All Access, HBO Now, Sling TV and YouTube are all serious competitors with designs on disrupting the traditional pay TV bundle as they increasingly fortify their offerings to compete for consumer's entertainment spend.

In response to the OTT subscription offerings, the incumbent MVPDs (multichannel video programming distributors) like Comcast and others are also disrupting themselves with OTT bundles that are similar to Dish's Sling TV. The cable companies have an inherent advantage of being the primary broadband provider, so consumers are already motivated to keep a subscription service with their cable company where they are likely already buying their broadband. Further incentives like exempting the data consumed to stream cable companies OTT offerings from their monthly data plans makes skinny bundles from their broadband providers a more attractive value. These new plans along with similar offers from wireless broadband companies like Verizon and T-Mobile to exempt certain streaming video and audio services from data caps are drawing the ire of special interest groups who may be competitively disadvantaged by these offerings. It is also attracting the attention of the FCC, who is the principal regulatory body charged with oversight of the internet and the enforcement of the current iteration of Net Neutrality and may ultimately intervene if they feel promotions are at odds with the intent of the Net Neutrality statute.

On-demand distribution is revolutionizing media, technology and commerce by providing more choice to more people at a lower cost with a superior user experience. Its impact on society is truly remarkable as great ideas in technology and media can increasingly be brought to life without the capital constraints that have always served as a gatekeeper. The principles driving the push to the cloud for enterprise software, database management and storage are enabling the new sharing economy. They also apply to media content and distribution resulting in a different paradigm for watching, listening to and reading news, information, sports and entertainment content. As business shifts to an on-demand model over linear distribution and to an access model over ownership of content, the consumer, the innovators and society will be the primary beneficiaries.

Applying the 4 C's framework of connectivity, convenience, choice and cost all speak to the value of on-demand content. Users want access to as much content as possible on any device at any time in any place. The popularity of services like Netflix, Hulu, Amazon and YouTube have been responsible for the drumbeat around the narrative of cord-cutters and cord-shavers. The existing Pay TV ecosystem will need to incorporate more and more on-demand content in order to remain relevant because appointment viewing is becoming anathema to the way people consume media with the growing options for on-demand content. In addition, it will be imperative that the traditional pay television distributor's set-top box, DVR technology and user experience continue to improve in order to keep pace with the OTT offerings from consumer tech giants like Apple, Google, Amazon, Netflix and Sony.

12 | A STAR IS BORN ... EVERY DAY

You probably know who Justin Bieber is, but you may not yet have heard of PewDiePie. What they both have in common is an early presence on YouTube. Bieber was discovered by Atlanta talent manager Scooter Braun through a talent competition video Bieber posted on YouTube while just 12 years old. PewDiePie is a Swedish-born comedian who also achieved fame on YouTube, but unlike Bieber, he continues to rely on the video platform as the primary distributor of his content. PewDiePie reached over 40 million YouTube subscribers making him the most prolific star on the digital video platform. He doesn't sing or dance, but rather he produces videos of himself playing video games in an emotive, highly animated style that includes yelling and joke telling. Gamers flock to PewDiePie's content, which is responsible for millions of dollars in new game sales and millions of dollars of ad revenue that PewDiePie shares with his producer, Makers Studio—a leader among online content aggregators known as Multichannel Networks or MCNs. The combination of social media and digital distribution platforms that operate on a global scale has provided content creators with unprecedented opportunities to build a community of fans and monetize their own brands.

Talent discovery can occur very quickly with the posting of a video that goes viral, possibly generating millions of views worldwide and supported with a significant presence on social media. A viral video can now generate enough buzz to put a content creator on the map, gaining the attention of producers and MCNs who endeavor to sign emerging content creators much the same way a studio or record label might do.

MCN is a loosely defined term for thousands of content aggregators who discover talent, largely through monitoring viral videos, and make investments in the individual content creators to help them produce, distribute and monetize their content. YouTube has hundreds of millions of videos uploaded to their servers, so an aspiring talent posting a talent competition video hoping to be the next Justin Bieber is akin to the proverbial message in a bottle floating in the ocean waiting to be found. There are hundreds of MCNs that range in size, scope and financial backing who aspire to discover the next superstar talent.

The role of MCNs is to provide content creators with much needed resources including funding, promotion, sales, rights management, audience development and content creation. It's the role that record labels play for musicians and studios have historically played for television and film producers. For the successful MCNs, it's another poignant example of value creation by co-opting the digital distribution channel.

Social media has become the most important marketing tool for aspiring content creators. Social networks like Facebook and Instagram, along with messaging services like Snapchat, Facebook Messenger and Twitter, are all multimedia platforms with a critical mass of users. Content creators and their promoters can post video, audio, text and images, which can then be shared to achieve exponential distribution—also known as going viral. It's not difficult for MCNs and other aggregators to troll social platforms to identify content that is trending with positive momentum and then seek out the producers for a representation deal or outright purchase.

Self-publishing is another rapidly growing digital distribution channel along with e-books giving exposure to aspiring writers. Amazon launched Createspace and Simon and Schuster launched Archway, both to make it easy for writers to publish electronic and/or print books through their platform, and there are several other independent publishers who have also launched similar services. It has never been more accessible or affordable for aspiring writers to publish and potentially become a best-selling author.

Contrast these new channels for talent discovery with either a band of musicians playing club gigs hoping to be noticed by an A&R scout who could sign them to a label, or an author who struggles to get the attention of an agent or publisher. The odds of a musician being discovered in the analog world—which required A&R managers to have a physical presence at the "gig"—were quite long. Today, the process of talent discovery is infinitely more efficient through social media and on-demand platforms. Both the acts as well as their fan response can be now viewed remotely in high definition video to evaluate artistic ability, performance ability and marketability in real time with social media metrics to gauge appeal and momentum. The net result is that more talent is being exposed to more A&R managers and is leading to more content being published and more ticketed live events. Content creators including filmmakers, actors, photographers, artists and writers all have access to these digital distribution platforms that enable them to expose their work to the world. It has created a virtuous circle encouraging more talent to emerge due to the increased exposure to content producers and distributors as well as accessible new opportunities to self-publish through social media and global distribution platforms.

The analog media ecosystem was an unconnected world filed with vacuums which created, by necessity, middlemen who acted as gatekeepers for content creators. Media companies were, in part, structured to serve as the gatekeepers between the content creators and consumers. Studios, record labels, book publishers, newspapers and magazines all served as essential distribution channels for content creators and used their leverage to extract a significant share of the economics. Distribution of content was a gating issue in an analog world, but the rapid emergence of digitally distributed media is helping content creators to find a home for their content, circumventing the exclusive distribution channels that were the province of traditional media companies.

Digital platforms reaching hundreds of millions of people combined with the democratization of production for audio, video, text and images has created an environment where it is now cheaper and easier to produce content, cheaper and easier to distribute content and cheaper and easier to monetize content. Moreover, digital technology-enabled virtual collaboration and content co-creation will produce art and science never before possible and will ultimately lower the cost of the creative process for Hollywood as well as Madison Avenue. The democratization of content production and distribution means that traditional film studios, recording labels, book publishers, newspapers and magazines no longer have absolute exclusives on talent and will find themselves increasingly competing with an expanded universe of digital distributors who will be aggressively vying for the best content assets and relationships with the most talented content creators.

Lastly, as content creation becomes increasingly democratized, it becomes more affordable, more plentiful and more customizable by platform and more personalized for individual consumers. The quality of user-generated content has moved well beyond the early pet trick videos on YouTube with over 300 hours of video being uploaded every minute to the site. Technology and skills have greatly improved enabling select content creators to compete with professionally produced content from established media companies. The lines are blurring beginning with bloggers, videos, music and photography. The combination of these factors will vastly increase the pool of content creators who will in-turn, create exponentially more content on every platform. Quality and quantity will both increase as distribution and production barriers continue to come down, so more talent will be discovered and more quality content will be surfaced. Expect the number of stars to increase and their natural duration to decrease as the velocity of the talent lifecycle increases. Andy Warhol's prediction of everyone achieving their 15 minutes of fame looks prophetic in the age of self-publishing with global distribution and promotion through social media platforms.

13 | NEWS IS A CAUTIONARY TALE

The business of news has been a very good business. Television, radio, newspaper and magazine companies have built media empires around the prestige and profitability of their news businesses. In the analog media world, news was consumed mostly by appointment as newspapers were published daily, news magazines weekly, radio newscasts in drive times and television news broadcasts at 6 & 11 p.m. Consumers were subconsciously conditioned to plan their day around news programming with breaking news being exclusively the province of radio and television broadcasters.

The traditional news ecosystem was first disrupted with Ted Turner's launch of CNN in 1980 which ushered in the 24-hour news cycle covering the news worldwide. It took several years and a great deal of both capital investment and operating losses for CNN to gain its footing and close the gap in quality with its network competitors. It was breaking news, however, that put CNN on the map beginning with the tragic explosion of the space shuttle Challenger in 1986, covered in-depth and nonstop by CNN. The network's next real introduction to the world was the first war in Iraq known as Operation Desert Storm in 1990 following Iraq's invasion of Kuwait. It was the first time a war was brought into people's living rooms through live television and it proved to be a game changer for CNN.

When the U.S.-led coalition began bombing Baghdad in January of 1991, CNN was the only television network with personnel on the scene. America and the world were riveted to their screens as CNN's embedded correspondents in Baghdad gave first-hand accounts of what it was like to be in combat supported by compelling video and audio of bombs exploding, tracer bullets whizzing, anti-aircraft guns blasting away. News would never be the same as people were now conditioned to expect real-time, on-the-scene reporting from breaking news events around the globe. The coverage truly put CNN on the map as an established news network and cemented their image as the go-to source globally for breaking news that they enjoy to this day. Ted Turner's vision created a new product category, which invited new competition. CNN pioneered the genre of 24-hour news channels, ultimately spawning competitors Fox News and MSN-BC which were launched as 24-hour news networks, and CNBC, Bloomberg and Fox Business which all compete as 24-hour business news networks.

In the analog model, news content was comparatively limited and filtered by editors constrained by legacy formats and beliefs in what is newsworthy—not to mention any potential ideological bias of editors or producers. Ironically, in its early days, CNN was criticized for reporting on stories that were unworthy of coverage as viewed through the prism of the nightly national news broadcasts. The old guard held firm to their belief that they were the arbiters of which stories were newsworthy enough to be presented to the American public and were able to fit the chosen content neatly into an evening broadcast that people would dutifully plan their commute and dinner around. If any of the big three networks in 1980 (ABC, CBS and NBC) had Ted Turner's vision for a more informed society through the power of live television, they could have easily launched a competing service using their vast resources or even purchased or partnered with him. It took 16 years, however, for another media visionary, Rupert Murdoch, to compete with CNN with the launch of Fox News as a 24/7 news channel.

MSNBC was also launched in 1996 as a partnership between Microsoft and NBC as a 24/7 news channel with a complementary online presence to create a connected experience between the cable television and online platforms. The concept didn't initially take root with the public and failed to attract a sufficient audience to compete against CNN. Ironically, the launch strategy employed by MSNBC was extremely prescient and would likely have worked well with Millennials who thrive on connectivity and multiscreen experiences. Differentiation based upon format and digital integration was viewed as a somewhat radical experiment at the time but turned out to be a harbinger of the multiplatform media model that is becoming the norm for news, entertainment and sports media brands in the Modern Media age. Interestingly, in both media and technology, the difference between cutting edge thinking and being a bit too early can truly represent the difference between tremendous success and a total flameout.

Alternatively, Fox News chose to compete against CNN with a uniquely different editorial point of view and distinctive presentation style that their Chief Executive, Roger Ailes, believed would resonate with a significant segment of the audience. Ailes' predictions were indeed correct and after several years of losses, Fox News eclipsed CNN in the ratings and has become one of the most valuable assets in Murdoch's media empire with estimates of over $1.5 billion of annual profits and the third highest revenue generating cable channel behind ESPN and TNT, both of which are driven by live sports. Regardless, the competitive battle between the two leading cable news brands has made both products better, driving large investments in their respective products as they compete for viewers, advertisers and sub fees.

The broadcast networks have all responded to the 24-hour news cycle by leveraging the fixed operations of their news divisions to create more weekly hours of news-related content. The additional programming includes expanding the windows of traditionally formatted news reports in the morning to news magazine programming premised on investigative journalism. Americans are getting their news in many different ways diluting the relevance of the vaunted nightly news broadcast in which the Nielsen-rated audience has fallen some

50 percent from approximately 52 million in 1980 to 26 million in 2015, but appears to have leveled-off over the past five years. However, the evening and morning news programs continue to be some of the most profitable programming content for the networks. News is content that the networks produce and own and can leverage a fixed cost investment in staff and bureaus across multiple news programs. Consequently, the cost to produce an hour of news is far less than the cost of an hour of high-value production entertainment. Furthermore, the news programming also contains larger inventory loads driving higher profit margins for the networks.

The economics and news consumption challenges are very similar for local television stations that are programming more local news content than ever in an effort to leverage their fixed investment in their news operations in light of increasing syndicated content costs and the potential exposure of too much reliance on network programming. More local news programming represents an opportunity for local television broadcasters to diversity their business model which has drifted somewhat dangerously towards being resellers of network content to cable and satellite distributors (MVPDs). Local news provides broadcasters with greater independence, local relevance and more inventory to sell at desirable CPMs as news viewers are deemed to be highly engaged viewers. Local news is also a magnet for capturing political ad spend, a growing revenue stream which is critical to local broadcast television's business model and news content is also ideal for building a strong digital presence driven by premium, exclusive mobile video.

Local broadcasters are also looking over their shoulders at their networks that are demanding an increasing share of retransmission fees received from video distributors including the cable, satellite and phone companies. The retransmission fees, known as "retrans" are expected to grow from more than $5 billion in 2015 to more than $10 billion in 2020 with some estimates showing even greater growth. As the networks continue to evaluate and experiment with direct to consumer (DTC) offerings, local affiliates are increasingly looking to their news franchises as proprietary content that ties them into their local communities, giving them more leverage with their distributors to increase retransmission fees from the roughly $1 per month per subscriber today. The projected growth of these fees by 2020 will depend upon the health of the pay television market and the continued popularity of local broadcast stations. Television broadcasters are in a two-front war, battling their distributors for increased retransmission fees driven by their "indispensability" while battling their networks who provide their content for an equitable split of the retransmission fees—also known as "reverse comp" in a nod to the legacy affiliate structure when networks paid the local affiliates to carry their programming. It's a striking example of the ebbs and flows of leverage within the media value chain of content and distribution.

For broadcasters, great local news programming is critical to driving better outcomes with both network and MVPD constituents, as well as driving higher advertising rates and increased inventory per hour versus syndicated or network programming. Local broadcasters continue to increase news programming as evidenced by the widespread rollout of news offerings beginning with the 4 o'clock in the morning time slot. It's yet another example of the continued expansion of news content in both traditional and new media. According to Pew, 68 percent of local television stations now program news for an average of 5.3 hours per day. The increase in television news content is smart business as it efficiently leverages the fixed costs of the news department and creates much needed online video content to power digital initiatives while building a stronger bond with local audiences and more opportunities for advertisers.

Local cable operators also understand the value of news and have been getting into the local news business by launching their own offerings or partnering with local broadcasters to create 24-hour news channels in New York, Los Angeles, Chicago, San Francisco Bay Area, Dallas, Washington, D.C., Seattle, Providence, Raleigh, Charlotte, Austin, Orlando and several other select cites. The trend is toward more television news content both nationally and locally as media companies continue to leverage their fixed investments in news operations. More hours on linear television and cable devoted to news content will lead to innovation through new formats and new features as programmers seek to positively differentiate their content and drive increased viewership. Consumers will invariably have more choice and convenient access to content across multiple devices. Moreover, the increase in high-margin advertising inventory embedded in news programming will benefit television companies' bottom lines.

NEWS IS THE FIRST DIGITAL MEDIA

The introduction of browsers like Netscape and Internet Explorer in the mid-1990s brought the internet to classrooms, homes and offices using dial-up services like AOL. It was also the very beginning of search engines, directories and web portals with the launch of AltaVista and Yahoo, also in the mid-'90s, that offered links to content sites found throughout the web. As consumers began to discover the web, they became exposed to a trove of more information and content than they ever thought possible. Early news websites included CNN, BBC and MSNBC and were designed to complement the television networks, though many staffers at the time were highly concerned about potential cannibalization. During those early days of the web, Bulletin Board Systems (BBS) enabled early users to have an interactive or participatory experience by commenting on posts in a threaded discussion.

At the time, most people didn't understand the potential of the web to disrupt virtually every industry, most notably media, technology and commerce. Just as the web was gaining momentum, however, the dotcom boom ended with a crash in 2000. In retrospect, a great deal of the fervor and momentum was temporarily shelved, but the underlying promise of the internet was largely unaffected. The web reinvented itself with more user-friendly features in 2002 including weblogs, now known as simply "blogs" and RSS feeds that begin to democratize web access. The collective feature set was dubbed Web 2.0 and ushered in a raft of new start-ups including Myspace, Google, You-Tube, Facebook and Pandora.

Similar to cable television in the '90s, it was a proliferation of content on the web following the dotcom bust that drove adoption and ultimately the confidence of marketers to invest advertising dollars in the yet unproven digital medium. News content (text and images) was the mainstay of the web with most newspapers putting their content online for free or having it posted through links by search engines and third-party aggregators. Consumers were being conditioned from the early days of the web that online news content was free and you only paid for the physical copy of the newspaper and magazine. This phenomenon rendered the "freemium" model essentially useless and only the publications with perceived exclusive content and a loyal readership that had the foresight to erect a paywall early on were able to train a portion of their readers to pay for content as digital subscribers. The Wall Street Journal and Financial Times both followed this approach and have successful digital subscription businesses. In an alternative approach, the New York Times has employed the freemium model better than most every other daily paper and continues to grow their digital subscription and advertising business, but with overall revenue and cash flow down significantly from peak levels in the middle of the last decade.

Bloggers were also gaining popularity as digital information publishing was becoming democratized. Citizen journalism in the form of bloggers was viewed skeptically by the professional media class, but consumers were more accepting of the both the content and the concept of self-publishing. The ability to access up-to-the-minute news online has caused venerable weekly news magazines like Time, Newsweek, BusinessWeek, Forbes and U.S. News & World Report to reinvent themselves by focusing their editorial on insights and analysis with their physical medium and more breaking news and short-form content and an increasing emphasis on video with their online effort.

As ad dollars begin migrating away from printed newspapers, it put increasing pressure on costs because the monetization of readership was at much lower rates on the digital platforms. The decline of display ad revenue for the local papers was exacerbated by the loss of classified advertising that migrated quickly to sites like Craigslist which offered a free alterative that quickly benefited from the network effect of users. The combined effect of declining display and classified revenue along with shrinking paid subscribers has created a severely challenged business model for daily newspapers. High fixed costs and declining revenue led to negative operating leverage meaning the reduction of operating profits is actually a multiple (leverage) of the decline in revenue. As a consequence, many journalists today are increasingly being compensated on the effectiveness of their content to engage readers and drive online revenue, which would have been a nonstarter during newspaper industry's halcyon days. In many newsrooms, reporters are now being equipped with analytics dashboards to track real-time engagement with content posts which, in turn, influences content production and helps determine their pay. Hard-hitting journalism that had been the raison d'être for the press for generations is, in some newsrooms, giving way to short-form stories of prurient interest that drives page views on a mobile device. The economic realities of print news journalism are hastening its decline because producing quality journalism requires a quality newsroom staffed with talented, professional journalists, but the business model no longer permits the breadth of coverage necessary to effectively report "all the news fit to print."

Since the introduction of the smartphone in 2007 to 2016, newspapers have shed close to 170,000 jobs and magazines have eliminated approximately 50,000 jobs due to the shift of ad dollars to digital media according to the Bureau of Labor Statistics. Jeff Zucker, CEO of CNN, famously coined the trade of analog dollars for digital dimes supported by the decline in newspaper industry revenue from a peak greater than $50 billion to less than $20 billion today and declining at a material rate.

Newspapers that served as the bastion of journalism for over 100 years now find themselves in a business where the cost to produce premium content cannot be profitably supported by digital advertising. Compounding the problem, the ancillary revenue streams of physical copy newsstand sales, physical copy subscription revenue and classified advertising are all declining at a faster rate than digital subscription and digital ad revenues are growing in nominal dollars. Newspaper business models are discussed in more detail in Chapter 17, but it's clear that consumer demand for content and ability to access it are greater than ever, but so is the supply of content and the attendant ad inventory making online news an industry in transformation as media companies experiment with different business models and cost structures.

In addition to the traditional newspaper and magazine sites, television and cable networks also actively leverage their global news organizations to publish content online. They are uniquely positioned to repurpose the plethora of video content they shoot for on-demand consumption to help them better compete against the dozens of free, pure-play digital news and aggregation sites including Yahoo, Google, Twitter, Facebook, Daily Mail, Huffington Post, Drudge Report, BuzzFeed and Business Insider. The proliferation of news content and aggregator sites correlate with the dramatic increase in news inventory both on-air and online, which has caused pricing pressure and margin compression for media companies. Even the most well-known, pure-play digital news sites are actually quite small media businesses in total revenue when compared to their national reach and it's believed that they collectively generate little or no profits calling the long-term viability of their business models into question.

The dramatic increase in both linear and on-demand news content has given consumers virtually unlimited choice and instant access to news. It has also changed the definition and scope of what constitutes news content as pop culture and celebrity-driven stories consistently generate high traffic and are becoming an integral part of broadcast, digital and print news content sites like Daily Mail, TMZ, Perez Hilton and Radar Online. These sites focus on celebrity-driven content often with a sensational, tabloid point of view and will benefit from the emerging trend towards live streaming of mobile video. They are extremely popular with Millennials who are spending less time with traditional news sites and have demonstrated a waning interest in core national and international news and government affairs. The multiple sources of continuous news from cable television, broadcast radio and online services have had profound effects on consumption patterns of both broadcast network news as well as local broadcast news leading to smaller, older-skewing audiences for the traditional broadcast programming. With virtually unlimited choice, consumers are curating their own content according to their needs and interests and consuming stories or individual pieces of content over a brand-first approach.

MOBILE HAS REDEFINED NEWS

Consumers now have instant access to weather, sports, news and information through a myriad of apps on their mobile devices. According to eMarketer, Americans are spending more than 3 hours per day on their mobile device up more than 400 percent from 2011. Approximately two-thirds of Americans now have smartphones and more than half of Americans use the smart phone as their primary source of news and information. This new and prolific behavioral shift is satisfying a basic information need that for decades was served by local and network newscasts and of course, by the print media. Mobile represents an attractive alternative for the consumer delivering on the promise of the 4 C's and is therefore expected to continue to supplant traditional, linear media offerings for news and information.

The ongoing challenge for traditional media like local television broadcasters is that the majority of their revenue and profits are still dependent upon selling 30-second commercials in the local newscasts. Newsrooms are becoming resource challenged as the ad-supported model is showing strains due to the falling value of digital and analog impressions because of an ever-expanding supply of available inventory and the increasing fragmentation of audiences. In order to remain relevant to both viewers and sponsors, traditional news organizations need to innovate legacy formats to create a more compelling viewer experience necessary to attract younger viewers with on-demand mobile content offerings. Broadcast news programming can no longer rely on audience flow and habitual appointment viewing to maintain or grow their audience necessary to drive ad revenue growth. All content elements should be reimagined including talent, set, graphics, show stacking, writing, production values and duration. It may require multiple offerings targeting different audience segments because consumers have been conditioned to expect a personalized experience with on-demand news content. This could be approached through an online channel heavily promoted to Millennials through the use of short-form segments interstitially placed throughout the linear content where targeting is optimal.

The proliferation of content is causing news to become commoditized, so product differentiation is increasingly based on POV. Mobile access has made news a real time, 24/7 cycle with online video offerings becoming table stakes for consumers. Mobile phones are not only content receiving devices, but are effectively becoming content creation devices with high-definition video and editing apps that enable a user to shoot, edit and distribute content from a smartphone. This exercise would have required a satellite truck and crew just 10 years ago and is enabling news organizations of all types and sizes to produce professional quality multimedia news and information content. Mobile technology including the ability to capture and stream video combined with the proliferation of real-time content across social networks and messaging apps including new platforms like Snapchat and Facebook Live are changing the way people consume news as well as changing the way they interact with content providers. It has also served to change the very definition of what is considered to be news because of the sheer volume of content being produced on a daily basis.

Consumers continue to be the big winners with real time connectivity and convenience, with increased choice and for virtually no cost. The 4 C's are indeed making news a top story in digital media.

14 | LIVE SPORTS REMAINS UNDEFEATED: NFL IS MVP

Live sports programming has become one of the few sure bets in content. It generates predictable ratings, particularly with men and Millennials, which are both difficult audience segments for marketers to reach. Live sports content has increasingly been in high demand by advertisers relative to entertainment content due to the high level of consumer engagement and the real-time nature of the viewing. Consumer engagement with sports is higher because people generally have an affinity for one of the teams or individuals competing and they are interested in the final outcome. It's the essence of being a "fan" that people root for their team, their player, their driver, etc., to win the contest and they are emotionally invested in the experience even though they are simply a spectator and not a participant. Marketers relish the opportunity to communicate with prospects when they are emotionally engaged the way people generally find themselves when they are watching or listening to a live sporting event.

The real-time nature of live sports also presents another important opportunity for marketers because not only is the context of the message positive, but the linear nature of live sports ensures that messages will be seen and heard. There is relatively no time shifting compared to non-sports programming because people want to see the games unfold in real time. Marketers buying linear television face an increasing dilemma as consumers watch fewer and fewer programs live and habitually skip the commercials during the replay. As media companies push for ratings credit up to seven days later, marketers are frustrated by their inability to reach people in real time. Awards shows for music and film, like live sports, are also valued highly by marketers for their engaged audiences and high percentage of real-time viewing to see who wins.

As the shift to on demand accelerates, marketers are facing the reality that their messages are being skipped-over and viewed as more of a nuisance thus making them less valuable. Entertainment programming doesn't demand real-time consumption the way sports and news programming does. The exception in entertainment is televised awards shows. The Academy Awards and Grammy's along with Dick Clark Productions' American Music Awards and the Golden Globe Awards make for highly engaged media events that are viewed in real time and have strong social media components that serve to heighten fan's engagement levels. These programs are the most similar to live sports content for fan engagement and real-time viewing levels. In addition, one-offs like final episodes of a long running, highly successful series will also be anomalous in the viewing public's interest levels and desire to experience the event in real time as with live sports programming.

The benefits to marketers from high levels of engagement and real-time viewing are fairly obvious. The benefits to the rights holders are often more opaque as they look for more ways to monetize expensive rights fees and amortize production costs. In most sports deals, programmers build shoulder programming content around the live games to take advantage of appointment viewing for pre-game and audience flow post-game to create additional content. Both pre- and post-game content leverages the draw of the games helping to offset the cost of the broadcast rights and production fees. Producing sports also requires a large upfront investment for production that necessitates multi-year rights deals in order to amortize the costs. Similar to the expansion of news content to leverage a fixed cost base, networks and local affiliates are expanding their production of game day previews and analysis with high budget productions to both entertain and inform the fans as they prepare to watch the day's slate of games and then re-gather afterwards to review the results and analyze the implications.

The pay-off for rights holders of live sports programming is the ability to command premium ad rates for the exclusive content. This is because the live sports audience tends to be more highly engaged with the content throughout the duration of the program block including pre- and post-game. A more engaged audience with the content is also a more engaged audience with the advertising messages. Marketers value live sports because it offers unique opportunities to create sports-themed campaigns that resonate more effectively with an engaged audience of sports fans. Many successful marketers produce specific campaigns for their sports marketing efforts to maximize fan engagement with their products. In fact, the Super Bowl is now celebrated as much for the football game as it is for being the "Super Bowl" of advertising campaigns as marketers pay the largest ad rates of the year to showcase their creative messages with the hope of generating social buzz to further amplify and extend their messages with incremental exposure or "earned" media. The "Super Bowl" of ads has become so important on Madison Avenue that entire teams are dedicated to creative projects a year or more in advance, charged with the responsibility of creating breakthrough campaigns which can serve as the foundation for the coming year's creative strategy.

There are dozens of sports leagues carried on network and cable television, but the largest four leagues—NFL, NBA, NCAA and MLB—account for the majority of the approximately $17 billion in annual rights fees paid by media companies to sports teams and leagues. Reflecting the strategic importance of sports programming, media rights are growing at a near double-digit rate and thus expected to reach $21 billion by the end of the decade.

Putting this number in perspective, media rights fees have roughly equaled the gate revenue at sports venues and are expected to eclipse it by the end of the decade. This is perhaps one of the most important "stats" in all of sports.

The team owners for decades were in the live entertainment business with a significant revenue stream from rights holders to broadcast their content. An important signal of the shifting economics in sports came in March of 2015 when the NFL eliminated their long-held blackout rule for local ticket sales. The rule had been in place since 1973 which mandated that a local game would be blacked-out if tickets weren't sold out 72 hours prior to game time. Its repeal speaks to the growing importance of televised live sports to the business models of both leagues and team owners.

THE NFL IS THE MVP — MOST VALUABLE PROGRAMMING

Live sports remain in high demand from advertisers because of the large and difficult to reach male audience they consistently deliver. Broadcast and cable ratings have been falling for years as the viewing audience fragments due to competition from digital, over-the-top (OTT) video. Conversely, sports programming has performed far better with the NFL accounting for ALL of the top 20 highest Nielsen-rated shows and 45 of the 50 most-watched shows of the fall season in 2015 with Sunday Night Football winning the prime-time ratings in all 17 weeks and Sunday afternoon claiming the highest overall ratings crown. There is no other sports or entertainment programming that comes close to the draw of the NFL as Nielsen ratings confirm the breadth and depth of the NFL's appeal, consistently outperforming all other live sports across all age and gender cohorts.

As an advertising vehicle, there is nothing comparable to an NFL game in terms of both audience and ratio of ads to programming. The average NFL game lasts slightly more than three hours and contains approximately 20 commercial breaks containing more than 100 commercials. The total commercial time is approximately 60 minutes or 1/3 of the game, which is considerably more than entertainment programs on television, which typically carry about 15 minutes per hour of commercials. The Wall Street Journal timed the actual plays of a football game and found that the average play lasted approximately four seconds for a grand total of eleven minutes of live football over the course of a typical game lasting 3 hours and 12 minutes!

Media companies continue to validate the strength of NFL's programming by bidding up the rights with each successive renewal. The current media rights deal runs through the 2022 season and represented an approximate 60 percent increase from the previous deal. The broadcast networks (CBS, FOX and NBC) are paying approximately $3.1 billion year with CBS' Thursday Night Deal reported to be an additional $300 million per season. ESPN is paying approximately $1.9 billion for Monday Night Football while DirecTV is paying approximately $1.5 billion for Sunday Ticket and Verizon is paying $250 million per year for mobile video streaming rights. Westwood One Radio Network, Twitter, Streaming and International rights make up the rest of the rights agreements.

As a harbinger of future rights negotiations, Yahoo reportedly paid $17 million for the exclusive rights to stream an NFL game in London. It was the first globally streamed NFL game offered free to anyone with a broadband connection through Yahoo's portal. The game was televised only in the respective home markets of Jacksonville and Buffalo, so all other fans had to view the game through Yahoo's stream. As the pay television bundle evolves, the streaming offerings, particularly for more niche sports or leagues will increase. The NFL sold the Thursday Night streaming rights on a non-exclusive basis to Twitter for an undisclosed sum, further demonstrating the strength of the league to bidders who are placing as much value on the association for marketing purposes as they are on the non-exclusive inventory which cedes pricing leverage back to the marketer buying impressions in the non-exclusive streaming content. Based upon the demonstrated value of the content, it should be no surprise that the media rights account for the majority of the NFL's total more than $7 billion of annual revenue with the rest coming from licensing, merchandise and national sponsorships. Live sports content could also prove to be a wise strategic shift for Twitter if they are successful in obtaining streaming rights from the NBA and other leagues as digital platforms compete for primacy in the lucrative arena of live sports content.

TO THE LEAGUES, GO THE SPOILS

Sports programming for the rights holder is a unique audience draw, but the economics overwhelmingly have shifted to the leagues. The robust growth rates in rights fees have far outpaced the growth of advertising revenue which has, over time, largely mitigated the profitability of the content. Networks continue to bid aggressively into thin or no-margin contracts because they need it for perceived indispensability with pay television distributors to keep the subscriber fees flowing. Digital OTT offerings are creating real alternatives to the large pay television bundle for not immaterial consumer segments. When a video distributor's large fixed-cost base is allocated against a declining subscriber base, margins invariably suffer. The result will be increased pressure to drop low-rated channels perceived to be non-essential when their carriage agreements come up for renewal. Exclusive contracts to distribute live sports programming may be unprofitable for rights holders, but can play a critical role in preserving pay distribution at profitable subscriber fee levels.

Another derivative benefit of sports programming is the opportunity to take advantage of a large audience to promote the rights-holder's non-sports programming which drives their profitability. Broadcast networks certainly don't permit each other to advertise on competitive networks, so the large audiences attracted by live sports serve as excellent promotional platforms to preview and promote the new television season and drive viewership for the important November and February ratings sweeps.

THE NEXT RENEWAL CYCLE WILL REFLECT THE FUTURE OF MEDIA

Live sports will continue to be a key content asset, but the economics and competitive dynamics of video distribution are inexorably changing. Look for the next cycle of media rights renewals to look very different with several new digital distributors entering the fray. The new entrants will be aggressively bidding for live sports content much the same as they are doing for news, television series and popular library content. It would not be surprising for large players like Netflix, Amazon, Apple, Hulu, Google/YouTube, AT&T or Verizon to bid for a rights package predicated upon exclusive video distribution through a digital OTT offering. Unlike the existing streaming and satellite distribution deals where the distributors take the feed of the networks, look for the new entrants to make the necessary investment in content production and shoulder programing to further control their destiny and enable them to innovate content and advertising elements.

Securing one or more of the NFL packages would be a game changer for any of the digital media companies looking to legitimize themselves as both a producer and distributor of sports content. It's analogous to Rupert Murdoch's audacious bid to take the NFL content from CBS in 1993, which effectively cemented Fox Broadcasting as the fourth broadcast network on par with ABC, CBS and NBC. Murdoch outbid CBS by $100 million per year plus the production investment to broadcast the games beginning with the 1994 season. It was unthinkable that a fourth network would be established, but the power of the NFL helped make it a reality. It's a good bet that history will repeat itself in some form when the NFL rights deals are up for renewal in 2022.

Consequently, the legacy rights holders will most likely be sitting across the table from a much larger bidding group at the conclusion of their current rights deals. To date, the NFL has spread the rights across the four major networks giving each major network an NFL relationship. This accommodation strategy can be overdone, however, if the content is too hard to find for consumers. The

NFL Network's airing of Thursday games was a prime example. Ratings were down materially because of both distribution and awareness challenges, not demand for prime-time football on Thursday nights. This was clearly evidenced by the increase in ratings for Thursday games when the package was picked up and produced by CBS in conjunction with the NFL network, which doesn't have the promotional reach to drive appointment viewing for the games.

The $10 billion question of the next NFL rights deals will revolve around exclusivity. By 2022, the perception of broadcast, cable, satellite, streaming and mobile channels—all of which have separate rights agreements in the 2013 rights deal, will have dramatically evolved with the paradigm shift to the new Modern Media. The likely delineation by this point in the future will not be predicated upon an analog distribution channel, but rather by just video and audio simply because the content and presentation is decidedly different between the two. When the next NFL rights deal is negotiated, the new economics of the pay television bundle should be sufficiently stabilized enough to understand the total economics behind a media rights deal.

Armed with the knowledge of how many consumers will likely subscribe to a sports package containing the games at a particular rate along with the expected value of the inventory will provide potential bidders with a baseline valuation of the content. Each potential bidder will then analyze the strategic value of the content to their respective platform based upon its ability to further their individual strategic ambitions within the context of their ability to fund the bet. The anticipated strong interest of well-capitalized digital media companies armed with their trove of data to better monetize the content could result in another game-changing bid for the rights. It's highly probable that the legacy rights holders will be up against multiple cash-rich digital competitors who will likely view an NFL rights deal as strategic and transformational and will bid accordingly. It's also highly probable that some or all of the broadcast networks will be well along in their respective online and direct-to-consumer strategies with incremental revenue streams and much more sophisticated viewer data to help maximize the value of their audience and compete aggressively against the digital distribution platforms to preserve their deals.

Netflix is already proving to be a harbinger as they have outbid traditional broadcast and cable networks for original programming and syndicated content. In order to compete, the broadcast networks will need revenue streams from both linear and OTT platforms. Content creation will also be innovated to incorporate more native advertising and sponsorship opportunities. More inventory through multiple distribution platforms will be key to funding a winning bid. NBC has demonstrated this playbook through their multiplatform coverage of the Olympics, creating more sales inventory as well as innovative cross-platform marketing solutions that increase fan engagement levels to drive incremental value for marketers. Innovating the content offering through linear and OTT/mobile platforms will also improve the accessibility and relevance of the content.

At their current growth rates, it's not inconceivable that Amazon, Google, Apple, Netflix, Hulu and Facebook could make aggressive bids in the next decade for key live sports assets to either drive device sales in the case of Apple, or fortify existing network ecosystems as in the case of Amazon, Google, Facebook and Netflix.

Video content distribution and audiences will both continue to fragment with the proliferation of on demand digital video, so live sports will be one the few opportunities for advertisers to engage with a large community of passionate fans in real time. As distribution silos fall, better-capitalized digital media and broadband behemoths like Google, Facebook, Amazon, Apple, Microsoft, Netflix as well as AT&T, Verizon, Comcast and Spectrum (Charter) will all increasingly compete for a platform suite of live sports rights across all of the major leagues. These potential suitors' enhanced digital and mobile distribution along with their financial heft will likely create a highly robust auction for the next round of rights fees and drive them to new record levels.

STREAMING SPORTS WILL ENGAGE FANS IN NEW WAYS

Digital distribution will enable content producers to innovate the fan experience in several unique ways. If the content is being streamed, by definition, it becomes a one-to-one telecast and can be highly personalized to the individual viewer if so desired. It will enable producers to create more personalized content for individual fans such as pre- and post-game interviews with their favorite players and coaches, even going to a more granular level where they may answer direct questions from their fans. Fans could also pick the stats they would most like to see as well as on-screen graphics—both design and content.

Multiple feeds could also be designed by individual users to show the plays developing down field as well as other teams' scoring plays in real time. There are virtually endless possibilities to customize a digital telecast for an individual user, which may help to expand the base of fans. Helmet and drone-based cams giving fans a realistic point of view of the action, in addition to bench and locker room cams to provide a more fulsome perspective of the game to enrich the fan experience could be integrated into custom, personalized feeds.

Fantasy sports will also be a beneficiary of digital distribution. Fans could receive real-time updates on their fantasy team with attendant video from key plays happening simultaneously across the league. Imagine four friends, each at home, playing fantasy football against one another where they can see each other, the plays driving their team's performance and real-time data scrolls on stats and scoring. It has the potential to create a far richer fan experience for not only fantasy players, but for non-gamer fans simply watching the game.

This technology is the province of the digital media companies, but the incumbent broadcast networks are developing capabilities and technology to execute all of the ideas proposed above and distribute them through an app either direct to consumer (DTC) or as part of an OTT bundle. Look for supplemental offerings in apps by the broadcast networks in the coming years to establish a toehold in digital distribution incorporating the content options of a multiplatform user experience including VOD, live streaming, personalization and commerce. By the time the various rights deals are up for renewal, it should be a considerably more level playing field regarding technical capabilities and product innovations between legacy rights holders and the digital distributors, not to mention that some of them may have merged by 2022. The deciding factor will likely hinge on the ability to monetize the content through a large subscription network or through more competitive ad models due to increased data and sophisticated ad technology.

Regardless of who wins the bidding contests for the next round of sports media rights, the economic leverage is accelerating its shift away from the rights holders in favor of the sports leagues and teams. The leagues enjoy protected monopoly status as rights holders to exclusive content that is highly desired by multiple distributors who are willing to sacrifice profits on the rights fees to win or renew the content. Understandably, the asymmetry of leverage in favor of the leagues is rooted in more of an auction than a true negotiation. Therefore, it's incumbent upon bidders to be creative in finding derivative or future benefits in the way they monetize a sports audience through both subscription and advertising revenue in order to justify stretching into a winning bid.

15 | VIDEO GAMES ARE SERIOUS BUSINESS

What generates over $25 billion in sales in the U.S. and has 155 million players of which almost half are women? If the video game industry wasn't your first choice, you wouldn't be alone. According to industry trade organization ESA, the video game business commands these eye-opening numbers, making it one of the fastest growing segments in all of media and entertainment. It was also one of the first interactive experiences in media as well as one of the first "platform" ecosystems with proprietary hardware and applications. Gaming has evolved to be both a participatory as well as a spectator "sport" and now has a multi-generational following, appealing to both men and women alike.

It all started with Pong, which was created in 1972 as a simple training exercise for an engineer learning to write code. The assignment was completed with such aplomb that Atari commercialized it as an arcade game and sales exploded. This began America's fascination with gaming. Also known as "interactive entertainment," gaming is surprisingly now in its fifth decade and has grown into a significant global industry within the media & entertainment sector. The interactive entertainment industry now consists of device makers who build the hardware and the publishers who create the games not dissimilar to the app ecosystem for mobile. Mobile has also impacted this previously closed ecosystem as the distribution of gaming content is now split evenly between devices known as "consoles" from makers like Sony, Microsoft and Atari which serve as proprietary gaming ecosystems as well as an emerging category of online games which are primarily designed for smartphones and tablets, untethering users from consoles to attract more "casual" gamers and widen the appeal to women.

Digital content distribution is having as great an impact on the video game industry as it is having on traditional media. Physical game cartridges previously sold through retailers GameStop or Amazon are now downloaded directly to the console, PC or mobile device. This translates into convenience and immediate access for gamers and higher margins for publishers. Brick-and-mortar retailers will need to evolve their business model to become more of a communal gathering place for gamers, selling products and services that complement the user experience because the content will continue to shift to a subscription model. Like music and video, gaming is moving from a product sale to a subscription or software's SaaS model—access, not ownership.

Another parallel trend impacting traditional gaming is social participation, which is enabling "gamers" to play with friends in casual games like "Words With Friends" and "Phrases," while other games are designed for serious gamers and offer a much more immersive experience that can last for days. Social gaming offers users the ability to form or join communities around a particular game or genre and has helped fuel the overall popularity of gaming with social games like "FarmVille," "Zuma Blitz," "Words With Friends," "Mafia Wars" and "World of Warcraft." Many are played through Facebook like "Farm Heroes," "Candy Crush," "Clash of Clans" and "Words With Friends," while others are played through console platforms like Xbox and PlayStation including "Grand Theft Auto," "Halo," "Call of Duty," "Minecraft" and "Fallout."

Gaming is the perfect content vehicle for communal experiences as it transcends boarders, cultures and language. In the offline console days, you could play with friends and family at home. Connectivity now enables gamers to compete against friends and strangers alike all over the world. It has become a true international sport, spawning leagues and live competitions that are selling out arenas around the world. The advances in technology and broadband networks now make it possible for so many gamers to play simultaneously that it created an entirely new category of games called MMO, which stands for massively multiplayer online. MMO's enable hundreds or even thousands of people across the globe to participate in a game like "World of Warcraft" where they assume roles and compete in a contest that might last several days. It's one of the most immersive and totally engaging experiences in media.

Mobile is another transformational trend shared between gaming and traditional media. The penetration of smartphones and tablets has greatly expanded the addressable market for gaming where over 150 million Americans engage in some form of interactive entertainment on a regular basis. For casual gamers, the smartphone and tablet have now become substitutes for dedicated consoles or controls with hundreds of thousands of game apps from tens of thousands of active publishers. Most of these employ a "freemium" model which relies on a small percentage of the app's user base to purchase virtual goods in order to give them an advantage as they play and compete. It's very much a hit driven business and the payoff is huge, so there is no shortage of new games coming to market to satisfy a large and growing community of enthusiasts.

The traditional distribution channel for gaming is the console with the market historically functioning as an oligopoly with Sony's PlayStation platform as the market leader followed by Nintendo's Wii and Microsoft's Xbox. Worldwide sale of consoles, however, are down approximately 50 percent from their peak of 90 million units in 2008 as gaming follows the rest of media content and moves more online through mobile apps. The number of choices combined with the ease of use when playing through a social network like Facebook make mobile gaming a more desirable alternative for the casual gamers whereas the hardcore gamers who play the console-based games will continue to play through the existing platforms but become an increasingly smaller segment of the overall gaming universe. Similar to music and video, console-distributed gaming content is also transitioning its model from ownership to access through subscription relationships with the publishers designed to provide a more balanced revenue stream for publishers while providing gamers with more frequent updates to keep the experience fresh.

Gaming is surprisingly mainstream as four out of five households own a device that can play video games and over half of households own a dedicated game console with over one-third of Americans playing some form of video games regularly for three or more hours per week. Its popularity certainly defies the commonly held stereotypes of the nerdy teenage boys holed up in their bedrooms. Today, the average gamer is in their mid-30s and they have been playing for over a dozen years. It's definitely more of a mainstream or mass market leisure activity as evidenced by the sales figures on major franchise releases. To put in perspective, only a highly successful movie will gross above $50 million on opening day. In 2015, two video game releases, "Fallout 4" and "Black Ops III," recorded sales of $750 million and $550 million respectively in their first 24 hours.

The gaming industry is evolving in lockstep with the rest of modern media as distribution shifts to mobile devices via broadband. Similar to music, the physical retailing of video games is giving way to online downloads. Video game content is moving towards a cloud-based subscription model which is designed to keep gamers more engaged with periodic updates and new add-ons to help users play games at more advanced levels. It will reduce the cyclicality of the business that has been dependent upon new releases that excite the gamers with a model to keep consumers engaged over a sustained period of time to generate recurrent consumer spending on virtual goods and advanced features.

Major publishers like Take Two and Blizzard Activision function like film studios who continue to exploit their existing franchises while looking for the next hit. Franchises are the most predictable source of revenue as evidenced by the sales figures for the fourth edition of "Fallout" and third edition of "Black Ops." Social games, whether they are hard-core action titles or casual titles like "Words With Friends," are fortified by the network effect which contribute to their franchise status. The games also consume a great deal of time, so it's difficult for most users to consume gaming content the way they may follow several different television series at the same time thus creating a real barrier to entry for new titles even though video game distribution has become much more democratized. As OTT television becomes more prevalent, beginning with commerce applications, it will take on interactive characteristics that will impact how content is produced. The delineation between watching television and playing games will slowly begin to disappear leading ultimately to one experience both in-home and away from home that will have continuity across screens and throughout the duration of an experience such as a show, a game or a sporting event and is seminal to the evolution of modern media.

SOCIAL VIDEO NETWORKS

Gaming is also ideal content for a social video network, which represents an emerging media growth segment targeting communities with a shared interest. Twitch, according to their published data, is the largest specialized social video network with over 100 million unique visitors each month who watch and engage with 2 million "broadcasters" as they play their favorite games and also provides a forum for fans to talk about video games with other members of the network. According to Sandvine, Twitch is already one of the top 15 most used apps overall with the service claiming more downstream bandwidth than the online version of HBO called HBO GO. Twitch's platform includes both live and VOD content targeted to the entire video game industry, including game developers, publishers, media outlets, events, casual content creators, and the entire eSports scene. Twitch has an enviable distribution advantage as its free live gameplay videos can be streamed from both Microsoft Xbox and PlayStation consoles which are the preferred distribution channels of passionate gamers.

RISE OF ESPORTS

eSports is an exciting new category that was borne out of passionate gamers' desire to watch the best players compete. With a fan base consisting of people who both play and follow the sport, eSports fans not only want to see an exciting competition, but they also want to learn new skills from the professional competitors to improve their own performance. It's a different fan experience and motivation from traditional spectator sports like football, basketball and baseball where the fans don't actually play the sport on any kind of a competitive level. Arenas like Madison Square Garden are selling out to watch pro gamers compete on a center stage with multiple video monitors displaying the action. It's creating an entirely new set of revenue streams including live events, merchandise, media rights and sponsorships with an addressable market that is global and growing very rapidly.

The pros compete in two primary leagues; ESL is the largest and MLG is the emerging competitor with more leagues likely to be launched. For now, the contests are centered around three games—"League of Legends," "Counter-Strike," and "Dota"—which account for the vast majority of eSports action in the two leagues. The fully distributed platforms which host these games make eSports a truly global sport playing to massive audiences worldwide due to the reach and impact of social media. There has never been mass global adoption like this in live sports due to the natural impediments of cultural barriers. eSports is also helping to bring gaming into the mainstream and represents a huge growth opportunity for the leagues and players as well as for the interactive entertainment industry.

GAMING WILL DRIVE ADOPTION OF VIRTUAL REALITY

Virtual reality (VR) has the best chance to find its way into the mainstream of modern media through video games, particularly the action-oriented console games. The serious, console gamers are already predisposed to purchasing hardware and would likely be interested in the incremental VR gear if it would materially enhance their gaming experience. The action games like "Grand Theft Auto," "Call of Duty" and "World of Warcraft" are all highly immersive experiences to begin with, but VR has the potential to create a lifelike sensation of being on the battlefield or in the speeding car. Obviously, VR will not be of high value to the casual gamers playing "Words With Friends" or "Candy Crush," but it will likely be embraced by hard core gamers giving the technology a strong chance to succeed.

The casual segment will experience a more immersive mobile experience through augmented reality (AR) which uses the location of the phone as well as its camera to provide a more real world context for content like video games. Nintendo's new "Pokémon Go" is the first major AR game release for mobile devices, which has the potential to bring AR into the mainstream. In fact, the level of immersion was so deep that police and transportation agencies across the globe were forced to issue warnings about playing the game while behind the wheel or walking on busy streets! Again, first introduced by games like "Pokémon Go," AR will be a major creative force in both content and advertising on mobile devices for media and marketers in the new Modern Media ecosystem.

Unlike 3-D, which never caught on much to the chagrin of television set makers, VR represents a quantum leap for immersive, action-based games. If the experience delivers as promised, gamers could serve as evangelists, which will help drive adoption and hardware purchases in homes across America. Once in the home, the VR device can be repurposed for alternate uses like sporting events, concerts and other forms of live entertainment as well as information and education. As with all new media platforms, content will drive adoption and there will also be enterprise adoption for commercial applications including training and simulation. This bodes well for the device makers and publishers who will evolve the existing console platforms, particularly Sony's

PlayStation where they, like Apple are competing as a vertically integrated media, entertainment and technology company to control the consumer's entertainment experience both in and out of home. Moreover, Facebook and Google are both making large bets on the transformative potential of VR and view it as possibly the next computing platform post-mobile, so look for continued innovation in both hardware and applications.

16 | SUBSCRIPTION IS THE PRESCRIPTION FOR DECLINING AD REVENUE

The subscription model is one of the most profitable in business as evidenced by the pay TV and wireless industries which generate approximately $100 and $200 billion respectively in annual subscription fees. The subscription model becomes even better when the incremental cost to serve a customer is virtually nil, as with media content or software such as Netflix or Microsoft's cloud-based Office 365.

Your mobile phone is likely on subscription plan where you pay a monthly fee to access the network of your carrier. Wireless carriers spend a tremendous amount of money to build and maintain their network, but the incremental cost of adding another user is quite low which in turn drives profitability and operating leverage. The key to profitability and increased shareholder value becomes customer acquisition costs, customer churn and the expense of core product development. The software business, which is primarily enterprise-focused has also been revolutionized by its shift to a subscription or SaaS (software as a service) model. Cloud technology has enabled software publishers to develop and syndicate applications to large user bases without significant incremental cost, but the applications need to be continuously updated to remain competitive.

Media is an even better subscription model than cloud-based enterprise software because content including books, movies, and music is basically evergreen, making it a pure syndication model where the content can be purchased or licensed and then sold over and over again. Bloomberg has over 350,000 subscribers for their content paying approximately $20,000 per year for access to the Bloomberg Terminal generating over $7 billion in revenue making it one of the largest subscription businesses in media along with ESPN, which also takes in approximately $7 billion in annual subscription revenue from pay television distributors. Both businesses are enormously valuable and have also proven to be highly effective and durable competitors.

Subscription offerings for media companies are becoming a strategic imperative as the economics of advertising continue to shift in favor of the buyer due to the ever-increasing supply of digital ad inventory combined with the rapidly evolving innovations in ad tech. A subscription component represents an incremental revenue stream for the ad-based media industry, which uniquely serves two core customers—advertisers and consumers. Digital distribution is making it possible to create completely addressable two-way customer relationships. This creates the opportunity to build a subscription paywall for publishers including on-demand subscription services for both video and audio as well as interactive entertainment, which has long relied on a "freemium" model by selling virtual goods to players. Important in this analysis is, first, who owns the customer and second, how does the customer value the content. The answers to both questions is generally determined by legacy business models and the success of early digital offerings in the space which serve to condition the consumer to perceived value.

For media companies operating with legacy ad-based models, the advertisers historically paid most of the bills and accounted for most of the profits. The consumers mostly received the product for free and in return, their end of the bargain was to read, watch and listen to advertisements designed to win them over as customers. This is how free, over-the-air broadcast radio and television existed for decades prior to cable and satellite offerings. Newspapers and magazines historically had dual revenue stream models where the consumer paid for the printed publication, which also contained advertisements. This dual-stream model wasn't possible for broadcasters as they delivered their programming directly to a consumer's radio and television via the public airwaves. Radio and television broadcasters were both originally chartered by the FCC to provide over-the-air service to the public free of charge, which of course, leaves advertising as their primary source of revenue, so unlike print media, broadcasters became solely dependent upon ad revenues from their inception. Television broadcasters, however, saw their business model evolve when they began participating in revenue sharing from local cable and satellite distributors, which became known as retransmission fees, but there have been no such fees for local broadcast radio which distributes their free over-the-air programming directly to the listening public through AM/FM radio receivers. There is also a distinct difference between radio and television regarding the way a local audience consumes their product. Broadcast radio's over-the-air signal is their primary distribution channel whereas only about 5 percent of consumers watch local television through an antenna on their TV set, but rather, they pay for it as part of an offering from their local cable or satellite distributor. Local radio and television stations are both broadcasters, with radio truly representing a free, over-the-air service to consumers.

Consumers' content options began to expand when pay television was introduced and became popularized in the 1980s. For the first time, consumers had the option to pay for television and receive incremental content they couldn't get from free, over-the-air broadcasting. This dual revenue stream supported the new cable channels like CNN, but was not shared with the local broadcasters until earlier this decade when broadcasters successfully negotiated for significant increases in the retransmission fees for allowing pay television distributors to include their content in the pay television bundle. Broadcast retransmission fees from MVPDs are expected to reach $6.6 billion by 2017 according to SNL Kagan while over-the-air advertising revenue for broadcast television is expected to be $22 billion. The second revenue stream of retransmission fees is highly profitable as it largely falls right to the bottom line because it doesn't consume any inventory and has little or no cost of sales.

Large media companies are aggressively developing strategic plans to become less dependent upon advertising. It's not unusual to hear the CEOs of large media companies direct investor's attention to their decreasing dependence on advertising revenue. As discussed in the previous chapter, advertising is a $190 billion market in the U.S. and growing roughly at the rate of nominal GDP, but the accelerating shift in ad spend to digital is causing a drag on the top line for traditional media companies dependent upon ad revenues. The antidote to an advertising dependent media company is selling content either directly to the consumer (DTC) or indirectly through a distributor. CBS, for example, smartly exploits multiple channels for monetizing their video content. For example, they were the first network to offer their content direct to consumer through a dedicated app while also selling select content to OTT services. CBS is also distributing its Showtime as a standalone streaming product through Amazon Prime who rivals Netflix for U.S. subscribers, both with over 45 million paying subs. Not all media businesses lend themselves to paid subscriber offerings however and will continue to be dependent upon advertising—both traditional and digital—for the bulk of their revenue.

Radio, unlike television or print, remains virtually 100 percent exposed to advertising because radio stations distribute their content directly to consumers through a one-to-many, free over-the-air broadcast license. Radio station owners enjoy a mass-market, installed base of receivers with over 270 million cars on the road and over 1.5 billion radios in the U.S. Radio broadcasters also benefit from high entry barriers to new competitors because FCC licenses are limited, but unlike television, radio broadcasters will be unlikely to benefit from subscription revenue for their core service leaving them highly exposed to the advertising markets. Broadcast television, as previously discussed, was similarly dependent on advertising, but now that over 93 percent of their distribution is done through a third-party MVPD which bundles programming for a subscription fee, the local broadcasters are now receiving as much as 25 percent of their revenue from an indirect subscription model which has provided welcome diversification from the ad markets.

In contrast, cable networks have long enjoyed a balanced revenue model between advertising and subscription. Like television broadcasters, their subscription model is also indirect, as the customer relationship exists with the MVPDs (cable and satellite) and they are paid a set fee per subscriber per month. Also similar to broadcast TV, the cable nets sell advertising in the national marketplace, but also allocate about two minutes per hour to the MVPDs to sell in the local market. In order to better compete for ad dollars against local broadcast television stations with full-metro audience reach that usually extends beyond any one cable franchise, cables systems have formed ad sales consortiums called "interconnects" to represent most or all of the metro households for the purposes of selling cable and satellite advertising. The MVPDs advertising revenues, however, account for less than 10 percent of their total revenue, so their core business is really subscription and they own the relationship with the customer. They also sell video, voice and data, with many now offering home security and even wireless mobility plans to maximize the value of each customer they do business with.

Large newspapers like the New York Times and Wall Street Journal with national and international readership have surpassed the one million mark for digital subscribers, with each generating approximately $200 million in annual revenue. One million subscribers, however, is actually a very small number in the context of Netflix's 70+ million global subscribers or SiriusXM's 30+ million paying subs. It's indicative of how consumers have been conditioned to value traditional journalism distributed online. Consumers perceive that news and to a lesser extent, music, are essentially free, but accept that premium video content is not. The implications of perceived value by content type will lead to further industry consolidation and investment as companies seek to diversify away from core advertising revenue.

Approximately 100 million Americans pay for video subscriptions with many paying for more than one subscription offering. For example, the majority of Netflix's 40+ million U.S. subscribers also subscribe to pay television through a cable or satellite distributor and/or are Amazon Prime subscribers. It demonstrates a belief by general consumers that premium video content is not free though they will still expect to view non-premium video content through YouTube, Facebook and Snapchat on a free, ad-supported basis. The market for music subscriptions, however, will more closely parallel journalism than premium video content. There are simply too many sites where free music is available to consumers both legally and illegally to drive mass consumer adoption of a pay model. Spotify's free, on-demand service along with YouTube, Pandora, Vevo and Vimeo give consumers enough options to create a free experience and tip the scales against a pay service for the majority of consumers, unlike video where they've been conditioned to pay for the TV bundle plus premium channels and movies.

SiriusXM represents a unique exception and stands out as the largest audio subscription business in the world with over 30 million subscribers and approximately $5 billion of subscription revenue. Its powerful model is to be a premium provider of news, talk, sports and music radio channels delivered directly to the auto via satellite. Unlike the on-demand digital music services, SiriusXM is basically a one-way "sat-cast" that provides exclusive and non-exclusive content to drivers with the music channels delivered without commercial interruption. For consumers, it's essentially a premium offering that complements the free, over-the-air broadcast radio they already have in their cars akin to HBO or Showtime complementing the pay television bundle. It's one of the very best subscription businesses in all of media because it combines the high barriers to entry and favorable content licensing rates of regulated broadcasting with the economics of top premium cable channels. It also has enormous growth potential beyond new car sales as over 80 million vehicles are currently not activated. The incremental cost to "light-up" these cars is low, so the SiriusXM model affords enormous operating leverage if they can implement successful content, branding and promotional strategies to drive greater consumer awareness and convert non-subscribers within their installed base.

As the Modern Media landscape evolves, look for more subscription offerings as media companies introduce DTC apps similar to CBS, Showtime or HBO. OTT subscription offerings like Sling TV, Apple, Netflix, Hulu and Amazon will spawn more competitors as consumers sort out their subscription video needs. Traditional pay television distributors will respond with more flexible offerings leading to skinnier bundles that make room for multiple subscription video products per household. Paid interactive gaming will continue to shift its model from transaction to subscription as social gaming becomes more mainstream. Gaming packages will likely be included in various OTT video subscriptions as an entertainment package beginning with console platforms like the Sony PlayStation.

Digital newspaper and magazine subscriptions will grow slowly against the headwinds of free content distribution through Facebook Instant Articles, content aggregators and messaging apps. Likewise, music will experience slow but steady growth in paid subscriptions with continued growth in free, ad-supported on-demand streaming. Artists will seek to maximize value by windowing their releases similar to the precedent set by Adele with her "25" Album which sold an impressive 4.5 million copies before being released to free, ad-supported distribution models.

Broadcast radio has a narrow path to participating in subscription revenue with its core business. Again, it's the only true broadcast model as television has long abdicated its broadcast distribution to the pay television ecosystem through cable, satellite and telco distribution. Creating unique content distributed on demand through podcasts represents the clearest path of leveraging radio's core competency of music curation and compelling audio content creation. Consumers will demand unique and exclusive content, but it's yet uncertain how large the addressable market is for an on-demand audio subscription service because as with music, there are thousands of existing free, ad-supported podcast options. Radio's subscription play will likely depend upon its ability to create and successfully market a subscription offering combining content, unique experiential opportunities and compelling offers for its listeners.

17 | REGULATION: FIGHTING THE LAST WAR

Regulation will continue to play a key role in the future of media. The principal regulators of both content creators and distributors are the FCC, DOJ, FTC and of course, Congress. Together they make and enforce the rules, which determine industry structure, rules of competition, resource allocation and consumer protections. Several key rulings and decisions will be issued in the coming years by these regulators that will influence industry structure, competitive dynamics, capital investment and the pace of innovation.

The last seminal piece of media regulation was signed into law more than 20 years ago as the Telecommunications Act of 1996. It was a landmark piece of legislation, which changed the industry structure for broadcasters by ushering in an unprecedented wave of consolidation. The world looked very different in 1996 as Google, Facebook, Twitter, YouTube, Netflix, Pandora, Spotify, SiriusXM, the iPhone and cloud computing didn't yet exist. When the legislation was drafted in 1995, no lawmaker nor lobbyist could possibly have foreseen what the world would look like in 20 years, particularly as we were about to enter the Digital Age—the most transformative economic period since the Industrial Revolution. In fact, this landmark communications legislation replaced the Telecommunications Act of 1934 which itself was passed before the advent of FM radio, television, cellular phones or mainframe computers. According to the FCC's website:

The Telecommunications Act of 1996 is the first major overhaul of tele-communications law in almost 62 years. The goal of this new law is to let anyone enter any communications business—to let any communications business compete in any market against any other. The Telecommunications Act of 1996 has the potential to change the way we work, live and learn. It will affect telephone service—local and long distance, cable programming and other video services, broadcast services and services provided to schools.

The FCC is charged with promoting competition, innovation and investment through the development, implementation and enforcement of telecommunications policy. The Telco Act of 1996 was sweeping in its deregulation of the telephone and broadcasting industries in addition to its early regulation of the nascent internet. For broadcasters, it increased the national cap for television station owners to 39 percent coverage and created an unlimited national ownership of radio stations with a cap of up to eight stations per market, which was increased from 2FMs/2AMs. In a nod to consolidation's opponents, the Telco Act disallowed cross ownership of newspapers and television or radio stations.

Telephone services saw perhaps the most deregulation with the Regional Bell Operating Companies (RBOCs) as well as new entrants now able to compete in each other's markets for local and long distance. This spawned the rise of the Competitive Local Exchange Carriers (CLECs) and long-haul fiber networks as companies raced to create the new "wired world."

Lawmakers recognized the internet as an important and emerging new way to democratize communications across an "Information Superhighway." As such, it was mandated that all schools, hospitals and libraries have internet access by the year 2000, while setting strict rules on child pornography and objectionable material online. Broadband did not yet exist, but is now an integral part of everyday life. IP audio and video were nascent while the emerging "peer-to-peer" networks that devalued intellectual property by enabling rampant piracy were not addressed in the legislation.

Under the Telecommunications Act of 1996, Congress well understood that telecommunications technology was advancing rapidly and provided for a periodic review of the Telco Act to keep it current with the advances of technology and needs of society. The first review was scheduled for 2006—10 years after the Act's passage—with the FCC obligated to complete a subsequent review of its broadcast ownership rules every four years, and repeal or modify those rules that are no longer necessary or in the public interest as the result of competition and new technologies. The Commission failed to complete its 2010 quadrennial review on time and announced it was combining that review with its 2014 quadrennial review, which the FCC finally completed in 2016 with no material changes—more than 20 years after the bill became law.

NET NEUTRALITY

Broadband—both wireline and wireless—have rendered legacy communications networks obsolete. The owners of the modern communications networks are comparatively unregulated, virtual monopolies. The cable systems control the pipe into the home and sell voice, video, data and home security in various bundles. They enjoy ownership of both the customer relationship and the leverage to encourage consumers to purchase a bundle of products, which are distributed over their network. As the cable systems aligned with content providers, some begin to favor some services that they had a financial interest in over others.

This prompted a huge outcry from content creators, distributors and advocacy organizations, which led to the 2010 passage of FCC's first set of rules to regulate internet access. After five years of court challenges, public comments and a rule making, the FCC passed the Net Neutrality rules designed to keep the internet open and free. The key provisions of the 2015 rule making were:

1. No blocking of legal sites—Internet Service Providers (ISPs) were not allowed to block any legitimate site

2. No throttling—ISPs are not allowed to intentionally slow data speeds for sites, nor speed them up for others

3. Increased transparency—increases the focus beyond the connection between the ISP and the consumer (last mile) to the rest of the net work to insure no special treatment upstream

4. No paid prioritization—ISPs can't prioritize sites by creating "slow lanes" for traffic on sites which don't pay a fee

Net Neutrality shines a light on the inherent conflict between broadband providers who invest to build and maintain high speed data networks and the content creators and distributors who "free ride" on the networks creating enormous value. Facebook, Google, Netflix and Amazon have all taken advantage of free and open access to build enormous value without the capital investment of the network providers. As bandwidth-hungry video streaming continues to grow, there will be increasing pressure on content distributors to subsidize network build-outs. Competition from wireless, incumbent phone companies and potentially even power companies will intensify against cable companies to make broadband service faster and cheaper as it becomes increasingly commoditized. The flipside of the argument is also compelling because the innovation required to create these beneficial services for society wouldn't be possible without the protections afforded by Net Neutrality. Lastly, it's also part of a larger effort by regulators to classify broadband as Title II (Broadcast Services) of the Telco Act in order to put broadband squarely within the jurisdiction of the FCC's regulatory authority similar to broadcast spectrum which could have future rate implications for broadband providers.

SPECTRUM AUCTION

The FCC will execute a major spectrum auction in 2016 designed to free-up valuable spectrum in the 600-MHz band for wireless broadband. The 600-MHz (pronounced megahertz) band is considered to be prime real estate for carriers because of the ability of the radio waves to penetrate buildings, which is key to providing a reliable wireless broadband experience. The rationale behind the auction is to repurpose spectrum which is a scarce resource for the greater good of society. Mobile data consumption is exploding while the 600 MHz currently licensed to television broadcasters is viewed as being underutilized because 9 of 10 consumers don't rely on the broadcast signal to receive their local television programming. Simply put, the spectrum allocations were originally architected in the 1930s and now need to be updated or optimized to maximize the utility of the public airwaves for the citizens.

Online video on smartphones and tablets is driving most of the increased demand, causing carriers to continue to upgrade their networks and maximize spectrum efficiency to serve their customer base. Optimization is a short-term solution, as increased capacity through spectrum re-allocation will be required to meet increasing consumer demand for bandwidth. The 2016 auction will most certainly not be the last as demand for online video continues to grow.

Mobile broadband requires ever more spectrum as carriers build-out networks to handle increasing demand for bandwidth to accommodate rapidly growing online video. According to demand forecasts from Cisco, U.S. mobile data traffic by 2019 will be equivalent to 220x the volume of U.S. mobile traffic 10 years earlier (in 2009). The explosive growth in mobile will require more spectrum with television broadcasters continuing to be the most logical place to source the valuable spectrum. The FCC plans to accomplish the reallocation and repurposing of some 600 MHz of the spectrum to mobile broadband by 2020 using a complex auction system.

The Broadcast Incentive Auction is comprised of two distinct phases. The first was the "reverse auction" where the government bid for spectrum and broadcasters effectively offered to sell their spectrum back to the government. It's an elegant way of repacking and optimizing the spectrum from the broadcasters they are using to serve a relatively small percentage of their audience in order to repurpose it for use as mobile broadband.

The Spectrum Auction enabled approximately 80 percent of the nation's 2,200 television stations to initially participate by agreeing to sell either all of their spectrum and simply taking the station off the air, or by offering part of their spectrum and continuing to broadcast by di-plexing or piggybacking with another local broadcaster. With approximately 9 out of 10 Americans receiving their television through a pay TV distributor rather than the free, over-the-air broadcast, it's relatively low risk for broadcasters to sell a portion of their spectrum into the auction and continue broadcasting on another local signal. Television broadcaster's "Must Carry" provisions and retrans fees will continue as will the existing channel mapping on their local cable or satellite distributor. Logistically, many television stations will have to relocate transmission facilities which requires capital and time, so the FCC will give the broadcasters until 2020 to complete their moves and deliver the spectrum back to the government.

The second phase, known as the "forward auction," is where the government auctions the spectrum it bought from the broadcasters to the wireless carriers who will deploy it as increased reach and capacity for their networks. The estimated proceeds from the forward auction range reached $80 billion with the bulk of the net proceeds earmarked towards national debt repayment.

The bids from the carriers along with the attendant build-out costs, speaks to the power of the subscription model for broadband services and the need for absolute scale to compete in such a capital-intensive industry. Moreover, if the 50 percent annual growth rate for mobile data consumption holds consistent, the industry will be facing bandwidth constraints once again shortly after the newly repurposed spectrum comes online in 2020. Look for a subsequent round of similar auctions with broadcasters and wireless carriers now that the current round is complete.

OWNERSHIP

The FCC regulates ownership through guidelines, which define limits around the number and type of media outlets one company can control in a single market as well as in total across the nation. They also control the amount of foreign capital permitted to invest in the industries it regulates though foreign ownership and foreign direct investment are reviewed on case-by-case basis. Given the amount of flexibility in ownership structure to create intended, asymmetrical relationships between economics and governance, foreign investment in U.S. media assets should be a source of capital and value for media companies going forward.

Cross-ownership has been one of the key areas of focus in the 2014 quadrennial review of the 1996 Telco Act which sought to eliminate television and newspaper cross-ownership in order to prevent a media company from exerting too much influence on the coverage of news and politics. Reread the last sentence and realize how much the world has changed in 20 short years. It's anathema to the way people get their news today for regulators to be concerned about a newspaper/television station combination. The FCC's rulemaking process is iterative and lengthy as evidenced by the 2010 and 2014 Quadrennial Reviews suffering such delays that they were not completed until the mid-2016 with the cross-ownership rules left in place much to the disappointment of broadcast and print media companies.

In addition to cross-ownership restrictions for newspaper, television and radio, there are also caps within each market for the number of radio or television stations one company can own. These caps were addressed in the original Act of 1996, but have not been updated to reflect the current competitive marketplace for audio and video entertainment and information. The one notable exception was the approval of the Sirius merger with XM in 2008 after a lengthy review. The two satellite radio services were originally chartered with the express provision that they not be allowed to merge, but were ultimately allowed to do with hardship playing a key role in the reversal. The SiriusXM merger is an excellent example of the role regulators play in the health and sustainability of an industry. Pre-merger, the two companies struggled to survive impacting their ability to invest in content and technology. Post-merger, SiriusXM is a healthy and durable business that has created billions of dollars of value for shareholders, with ample resources to invest in content, people and technology.

The combined entity has given consumers an excellent premium audio-sub-scription service to complement local broadcast radio. As ad dollars continue to shift to digital, look for the FCC to address ownership caps—both locally and nationally—in the 2018 and 2022 Quadrennial Reviews. In lieu of regulatory relief, broadcasters may also challenge the existing rules through a proposed mergers similar to the strategy employed by Sirius and XM.

PRIVACY ISSUES

Social media is, by its very nature, somewhat at odds with privacy. Social media's raison d'être is to provide a platform for its users to be social by sharing much of their lives online. However, as many people have learned, information including photos or videos that one might be comfortable shar-ing with friends may be inappropriate or even detrimental if reviewed by a current or prospective employer.

The ability of employers trolling social media to learn more about their current or prospective employees is a hotly debated legal and ethical issue across the workplace. State lawmakers are tackling the issue with dozens of laws that restrict the ability of employers or academic institutions to ask for passwords. Some industries like financial services have compliance laws that mandate that employee communications including social media be monitored so the issue of privacy is highly nuanced.

In media, the issue of privacy also extends to the relationship between users, publishers and marketers. It creates an inherent conflict of interest be-tween platforms who benefit from information and their ability to market it and users who, for the most part, don't understand how much personal in-formation they abdicate daily to publishers through tracking their online be-havior. This goes beyond exercising judgment about what to post on a public forum like Facebook or Instagram and is core to the business model of the online advertising industry which is predicated on serving smart ad impressions derived through otherwise confidential demographic and consumer behavior information. The FTC is charged with protecting the public, but the lengthy disclosure obligations found in apps are rarely read when routinely accepted making consumers willing accomplices in the collection and marketing of their personal data.

CONSOLIDATION AND MARKET DEFINITION

The DOJ and FTC are the principal regulators on media mergers and acquisitions and they work in conjunction with the FCC to insure that deals both comply with the existing rules and are pro-competitive. Rules like the Telco Act of 1996 are practically outdated by the time they are enacted, let alone having any material relevance 20 years later. Moreover, the last 20 years have witnessed the most profound changes to the competitive landscape for media and telecommunications in history, rendering most of the act irrelevant in today's hyper-competitive marketplace.

Consolidation through mergers and acquisitions is an effective way of enabling legacy companies and industries to remain viable. Outdated industry structures must be allowed to reformulate through combinations that may help eliminate irrational competition leading to price wars that invariably lead to underinvestment and ultimately result in extinction. Regulators can play a constructive role in allowing the market to function in order to protect an industry from mutually assured destruction due to irrational pricing as they did when reversing course on the satellite radio merger.

The key lever for regulators is market definition. If a market is defined too narrowly, an objective view of "pro-competitive" will be too conservative and proposed transactions will either be denied or approved with onerous conditions that negate the industrial logic of the deal to begin with. This is the most important reason for adopting an up-to- the-minute viewpoint of the competitive dynamics of the marketplace. For example, the advertising markets are inexorably moving towards impression-based buying. All advertising inventory will eventually be normalized as "impressions" and thus converting from metrics like "Gross Rating Points (GRPs)," "Monthly Uniques," "Average Quarter Hour" (AQHs) and Cume. This will require a wider view of markets, which are no longer siloed as advertisers seek to buy impressions using programmatic ad buying technology to maximize the ROI. Buyers have infinitely more choices today to fill their needs, so what may have seemed like a rational "market" structure for traditional media just 10 years ago is no longer viable today. Broadcast television and radio both are in fierce competitive battles for local and national advertising as the substitute products for local buyers have now expanded to Google, Facebook, Pandora, YouTube, Hulu, Spotify, Yelp, Autotrader and Cars.com as well as a host of digital ad networks.

Media regulators have an important and difficult task as the digital transformation continues to disrupt and reshape markets and industries. They have both the responsibility and challenge to evaluate combinations based upon the true realities of the current marketplace and be cognizant of inexorable trends that may make certain combinations absolutely necessary in the very near future. The role of the regulators is to promote competition and innovation while protecting consumers. By nature, regulators react to existing conditions and events rather than anticipate what will likely happen during the effective period of any new policy. Combine a lengthy and reactive policy development process with a rapidly changing traditional and digital media marketplace and the result is antiquated regulation that handcuffs our civil servants and relegates them to perpetually fight the last war.

18 | REMAKING TRADITIONAL MEDIA: CONTENT, DISTRIBUTION & MONETIZATION

Think of a media ecosystem as an interconnected web of businesses, which participate along the value chain from content production to content distribution and monetization. It's an end-to-end series of businesses and processes, which enable the ongoing creation and consumption of media content. The new digital ecosystem has seen the emergence of new content creators in music, video and journalism, as well as new distributors ranging from YouTube, Amazon, Hulu, Spotify, Apple and Facebook. The advertising component of the new digital ecosystem has witnessed perhaps even more change as the entire process of buying and selling advertising has been upended because of individual addressability and the newfound ability to dynamically serve ads.

Traditional media companies are grappling in real time with the impact of the new digital media ecosystem and the accelerating shifts in consumer behavior, which threaten to upend legacy business models and cultures that were galvanized in a much less competitive world. The creation of a new digital media ecosystem over the last 10 years threatens to subsume the legacy media ecosystem that has been the exclusive province of traditional media and advertising companies. The next 10 years will witness the combination or convergence of the two existing ecosystems into a new, Modern Media ecosystem where distribution is principally IP-based with broadcast and satellite radio being the notable exceptions.

Today, the leverage, power and economics in content, distribution and advertising are shifting faster than most thought possible. As a result, the new competitive realities are having profound impacts on the viability of individual companies as well on the industries in which they compete. Over-the-Top (OTT) subscription services like Netflix and Amazon Prime are aggressive bidders for content, which serve to drive up costs for traditional buyers like broadcast and cable networks. Google and Facebook are capturing significant ad share and the massive amounts of digital impressions they are bringing to market are putting pressure on traditional ad rates. Free, ad-supported streaming services like Spotify and YouTube are significantly cannibalizing digital downloads from iTunes, which previously had decimated the physical sales of CDs prompting Apple to shift their business model in music to a subscription service (Apple Music) from a transaction model through the iTunes Store.

The New Modern Media ecosystem will be structured around the content foundation of traditional media, but fully leverage technology to distribute and monetize content in a more personalized way. The current struggle between legacy and new media will eventually fade as the new modern model takes root. Existing media segments and companies will be impacted differently, and how they compete over the next several years will determine their survival and durability as they endeavor to evolve legacy business models to compete successfully.

CONTENT, DISTRIBUTION & MONETIZATION: A STRATEGIC FRAMEWORK

Analyzing the future prospects of legacy media industries requires a cogent understanding of the role each plays in the media ecosystem's value chain. As a corollary, all media companies play in either content, distribution or both; and all media companies have to monetize (sell) their content directly to the consumer or distributor, or indirectly, by monetizing their content through the sale of advertising. The digital media ecosystem tends to impact or disrupt distribution and monetization more than content creation because successful content creation will always be an art form, which is highly skilled, requires talent and is subjective. Distribution, however, can much more easily be automated and optimized by machines, which in some cases may render companies or entire industries irrelevant and even obsolete.

Traditional media businesses could benefit by employing a strategic framework against content, distribution and monetization (CDM) to determine each business' source of value and expected durability in the new post-digital, Modern Media world. It's a given that the media landscape will look different throughout the next decade than it does today and look considerably more different again by 2030. The innovation spurred by digital technology and mobile apps & devices has forever changed the way society works, lives and interacts. The years leading up to 2020 will be instrumental in shaping the future prospects of both traditional and digital media companies as many of the new, rapidly growing media sectors like social, online video and messaging will become more mature. Conversely, traditional segments will continue to evolve—particularly the distribution businesses—with consolidation playing a key role in the reconfiguration process. The principles of industrial Darwinism will apply and success, or even survival, will depend upon a specific industry's ability to adapt to the intense competitive pressures being felt by the digital media disrupters across the spectrum in content, distribution and monetization.

CONTENT CREATION IS BECOMING DEMOCRATIZED

Silos no longer exist and consumers now consume media from multiple platforms. Digital has made it easier to record a song, shoot video and certainly to produce text and images. Content is also increasingly user-generated, as anyone can become a digital content publisher today. Social media and messaging platforms are consuming a significant amount of time spent with mobile devices and facilitating the emergence of new stars on YouTube, Instagram, Facebook, Snapchat and Twitter. We've all heard the phrase in the media business that "content is king." It's analogous to "location, location, location" in real estate. Creating and distributing quality content—much the same as securing a great location for a building—insured success. This made perfect sense because great content has always created leverage with distributors driving better economics for the content owners. Content will always be the critical determinant in success because it's the product, but the equation for creating value has now changed.

Content has traditionally been held captive to rigid distribution channels like newspapers, radio stations, television and cable networks. Newspapers and magazines decide when and where to run stories and editors make decisions about an article's length to fit within a form—sometimes at the expense of a great piece of content. Ad-to-edit ratios also play a role in what content is published in print media, again creating leverage for the distributor. In electronic media, broadcast and cable network programmers have historically worked in a linear medium and regularly make tactical decisions on program scheduling to benefit nascent or even struggling content by leveraging the audience flow from popular programs. Radio station programmers have long had the power to break and make hit records as well as the acts behind them. Without that key part of the distribution channel, most musicians could never get out of the clubs. Content in both print and electronic media, including music, journalism and filmed entertainment is being liberated as static forms and linear formats are gradually being replaced in the digital age with on-demand technology.

Content products and services are also changing with technology and consumer behavior. Consumers want different types of content depending upon their activity and device. They may want to listen to music on demand, watch videos, play games, read a newsfeed, make a social post or share content through a messaging service. In addition, the notion of appointment viewing or even viewing as a singular activity is anathema to how people consume media—particularly Millennials. As in most industries, innovators and disrupters are the challengers and are often the catalysts for change, but don't participate ratably in the economics because new business models tend to lag behavioral change. The time spent with online video versus the ad share captured is a prime example of the lag—with television capturing $70 billion of ad revenue versus an estimated $10 billion for online video in 2016. Incumbents are powerful and difficult to dislodge because they have exclusive assets, skills and industry knowledge. In addition to their experience, incumbent content creators have access to talent as well as key distributor relationships. They also have access to capital and leverage over the value chain, as well as the ability to match competitive offerings.

DISTRIBUTION IS DRIVING DISRUPTION

The most significant change in media has occurred on distribution side of the house. As detailed in Chapter 7, The Distributor's Dilemma, distribution in media is everything that happens between content creation and content consumption. Often, content passes through multiple distributors before reaching the end consumer. For music, distribution begins with the record label followed by the digital distributor like iTunes or Spotify or the physical retailer like Target or WalMart. For a television show, it's a producer followed by a studio, followed by a network like CBS or USA, or a syndicator selling to a local station, or a digital streaming service like Netflix or a physical copy (DVD) sold at retail by WalMart or online by Amazon.

In the digital media ecosystem, distribution has become more de-siloed in the last mile to the consumer as digital content is reduced to "bits" so voice, video, audio, text and images are all transmitted across the same networks and can be processed by the same devices. Your phone, tablet, laptop or PC is now also a radio, TV, gaming console, newspaper or magazine. According to Pew Research, almost two-thirds of Americans have smartphones and people are engaging with their devices throughout their waking hours, spending more than three hours per day consuming content on their smartphones. The last mile to the consumer for most content distributors is now through the smartphone making mobile an imperative for any content distribution strategy.

Digital distribution at scale for content and commerce is inherently democratic with no initial barriers to entry, but the door closes fast behind first movers who execute successfully due to the network effect as evidenced by Amazon, Netflix, YouTube, Hulu, Pandora, Spotify, LinkedIn, Uber, Airbnb, Google, Facebook, Snapchat and Twitter. What these digital distributors of media and commerce all have in common is a relative first mover advantage and the network effect. Traditional media distribution businesses like newspapers, television networks, record labels, publishing houses and movie studios are all, to varying degrees, trying to figure out how to compete with, partner or buy the digital distributors who have built and scaled powerful businesses right alongside the incumbents achieving critical mass and emerging as competitive threats.

Much of this book has explored how and why the digital transformation has so fundamentally impacted traditional media, including an enormous value transfer to the new digital distributors who operate at scale. For example, Facebook is quickly becoming a major distributor of news and video content without producing, buying or licensing the content itself. In an effort to drive traffic and near-term revenue, publishers are ceding both primary distribution of their content as well as the customer relationship which could have a dilutive impact on their brands over the long run. Moreover, Apple, Netflix and Amazon Prime have all become key distributors for producers selling music, film and television, spending billions on hardware and data centers as ecosystems are being built around these companies leveraging both the "network effect" of their digital platforms and the scaled infrastructure scale necessary to deliver the product on demand to tens of millions of customers.

The evidence clearly indicates that a fundamental platform shift is well underway from analog or physical distribution to digital that leaves few alternatives for legacy distributors in their current form. The required shift to digital is not in question, but the ability to maintain a legacy market position as a new digital distributor is far from guaranteed. This is particularly true for newspapers, magazines and record labels and to a lesser extent for local television stations who have long relied on the local pay TV distributors and have never directly owned the customer relationship. When analyzing the prospects and strategic plans for traditional media companies, distribution as a primary source of value can be a key strategic vulnerability.

MONETIZATION

There's an old and wise adage in business: Nothing happens until you sell something. The way media businesses monetize (sell) their product is also changing rapidly in the context of the digital media ecosystem and in many cases disrupting legacy business models. From content creator to consumer, transactions occur all along the value chain, and some value chains are longer and more complex than others. As a rule of thumb, the more transactions that occur between the producer and the consumer, the greater the potential for disruption and optimization. Media companies have historically enjoyed such high margins because they controlled their distribution and used it as a high barrier to entry to limit competition and drive high operating margins. For example, the classic newspaper model was to produce the content in-house, print the content in-house and distribute the content to homes and business through their delivery network, which was again, in-house. On the B2B side, they sold their ads with an in-house sales team and produced the copy with another in-house team. Whether it was selling to the reader or the advertiser, the newspaper was vertically integrated, controlling its content, distribution and monetization end-to-end. Historically, newspapers enjoyed profitable and protected business models until they lost control of their distribution as it shifted from physical to digital.

As the newspaper example illustrates, many media businesses have revenue streams from both consumers and advertisers. Analyzing a media business' ability to drive revenue and, ultimately, profits requires a deeper look into fundamental trends of both revenue streams including: Market growth, pricing, share of addressable market and marginal contribution.

The ability to drive pricing power comes back to the basic economic tenet of supply and demand. The new digital media ecosystem has created an almost infinite supply of new inventory known as "impressions" while constant innovations in ad technology are making it easier for marketers to access and aggregate the vast supply of "smart" impressions in real time.

Traditional ad-based media companies are grappling with revenue growth because pricing power has been eroded due to the imbalance of supply exacerbated by the demand for smarter impressions as marketers work to improve targeting. This creates an environment where advertising revenues will grow more slowly than trend as marketers leverage ad technology and digital marketing platforms to serve smarter ads. For marketers, the prospect of spending less and achieving more creates an opportunity to compete more effectively on price in the marketplace without sacrificing their marketing competitiveness. This same basic supply and demand trend is happening in transportation and lodging as inventory and accessibility expand arithmetically through digital distribution services like Uber and Airbnb and also by the imitators they spawn.

The revenue growth rates of digital media distributors like Facebook and Google are driven by volume growth in premium segments, not pricing. In other words, the growth in impressions they are taking to market far exceeds the decline in pricing due to increased supply and innovations in ad technology. Conversely, Yahoo has reported revenue declines for several consecutive years in spite of taking more inventory to the market through content acquisitions and new product launches. The pricing decline in the non-premium "display" segments has been greater than Yahoo's increase in impression volume accounting for their persistent revenue declines.

Pricing trends for advertising impressions will most likely be deflationary as digital distribution and ad tech will enable advertisers to identify and address virtually every consumer. Moreover, as consumption continues to shift to mobile, marketers will be able to amass large target audiences through a build-up of individually targeted impressions. With the exception of unique, exclusive content assets like the NFL, the Academy Awards or the Grammy's which will likely maintain pricing power, the conventional ad revenue segment for media companies will need to grow through increased volume rather than pricing. Consequently, media companies will be driven to innovate their ad products with solution-based, integrated digital offerings to complement their core in-program commercials.

MARKET OPPORTUNITY

An important component of monetization analysis is the realistic addressable market. The creation of the digital media ecosystem in parallel with the existing traditional media ecosystem is very similar to what has been occurring in retail with the primary difference being retail's capital intensiveness. Facebook, Google/YouTube and Netflix all require a fraction of the capital investment to digitally distribute content at scale compared with what Amazon requires to operate at scale which is a massive physical distribution network. Yet in both media and retail distribution, only a few players dominate with a very long tail of niche competitors. For traditional media companies or aspiring new digital entrants, the true addressable market varies greatly by segment and is determined by the strength and tenure of the market-leading incumbent. Network effects, access to capital, ownership of the customer, perceived switching costs and leverage across the value chain all work in concert to determine the true addressable market for a distributor.

The fastest growing segments in media are mobile, online video and subscription services. Online advertising is growing double digits with estimates as high as $100 billion in 2020. By inference, non-digital advertising is then shrinking. Consumers are spending more time with their mobile devices and they are becoming the primary way people consume media, communicate with others, bank, shop and manage their daily activities.

Advertisers follow consumers and they now have an opportunity to communicate with them not only while they're consuming media, but while they're living their daily lives. The conundrum for most media companies is the execution risk and potential cannibalization of a high-margin core business by driving consumers to rapidly growing digital distribution platforms. For newspapers and magazines, moving readers to digital distribution without first establishing its value, has not proven to be a good trade and serves as a useful predicate for radio and television stations that rely on advertising as their principal revenue stream.

Subscription services are growing as more offerings come to market for movies, television shows, television channels, music, radio, podcasts, gaming, newspaper paywalls and passion points like pets, gardening, cooking, fitness, etc. With the exception of radio broadcasting, consumers have historically paid for content packaged as movies, television, books, records, tapes, newspapers, magazines and game cartridges. The re-ordering of the media distribution ecosystem combined with the shifting economics of free, ad-based monetization models are compelling media companies to more aggressively develop, offer and market subscription services.

BUSINESS MODEL

Successful media business models all enjoy high marginal contribution, which is the profitability of each incremental dollar of revenue generated. Low variable costs per dollar of revenue booked are the key to high marginal contribution where volume translates into profit and building scale usually results in enormous value creation. Prime examples are syndication or subscription businesses where content is produced once and then duplicated inexpensively and resold at a very high gross margin. Once the fixed costs are covered, each incremental dollar of revenue flows to the bottom line at a very high conversion rate. This is known as operating leverage and is a very positive attribute for any business model. Digital content can be reproduced at virtually no cost so the key determinant for true marginal contribution from digital syndication or subscription businesses are customer acquisition costs and content rights fees.

Most costs our fungible, so the high marketing costs to acquire and retain customers serve to reduce marginal contribution. Moreover, a business model with high variable costs for each incremental dollar of revenue like the music streaming services can actually result in negative contribution if the combination of marketing and rights fees are onerous enough. It reminds one of the old saying that "we're losing money on every sale, but we'll make it up in volume!"

Business models with high variable costs can be either structural due to high rights fees for content or they can be operational due to high customer acquisition costs, high turnover or a combination of both. Distribution costs for content can also create high variable costs for physical media such as premium-quality magazines which are expensive to print and mail, often far exceeding the cost per subscription, thus relying on incremental advertising and event revenue to create a business model with positive marginal contribution for each additional subscriber.

APPLYING THE CDM FRAMEWORK TO TRADITIONAL MEDIA

A critical look at current media landscape—traditional and digital—including television, radio, recorded music, newspaper, magazine and gaming using the CDM framework is helpful to determine which industries and companies are best positioned to evolve and compete successfully into the next decade beginning with television.

Traditional television has seen significant audience erosion by younger viewers in the five-year period from 2011 through 2015. According to the Nielsen Total Audience Report, teens are watching 30 percent less television with

Millennials watching 24 percent less television and Gen Xers watching the most of the three cohorts, but still down 11 percent during the four-year timeframe. They're watching less traditional television, but more video overall with the explosion of OTT digital video from Netflix, Hulu and Amazon Prime, as well as user generated content from YouTube and Facebook.

In spite of declining audience, television has managed to hold pricing by increasing CPM (cost per thousand) rates due to continued, strong advertiser demand for large, real-time audiences. The traditional television ecosystem includes broadcast networks, local TV stations, cable networks and MVPDs, while the new digital video ecosystem adds OTT platforms, multichannel networks (MCNs), DTC channels as apps and user-generated content (UGC). The merging of the two ecosystems is in the early stages, but will look quite different in the next decade as the new Modern Media ecosystem begins to take shape. The CDM framework is an instructive way to predict likely outcomes and determine the fate or fortune of the various components of the quickly evolving television and digital video ecosystems.

LOCAL BROADCAST TELEVISION

Local TV is perhaps the most enigmatic business in media. It produces and owns content in the form of local news and licenses content from syndicators in the form of daytime talk and game shows. It also functions as a middleman by distributing content on behalf of national broadcast networks ABC, CBS, FOX, NBC and others for which it pays "reverse comp" back to the networks and keeps a portion of the commercial inventory to sell into the local and national spot marketplace.

Broadcast television's most lucrative content is its local news because it has the highest ratio of ads-to-content with all the inventory owned by the local station and newscasts also command premium ad rates because news programming is more likely to be viewed in real time, making it more highly valued by advertisers. Political advertising is another derivative benefit of increased news programming. News inventory represents the most desirable programming for political ads because news viewers have a higher level of engagement with the content and are more likely to show up at the polls.

Following a period of decline, as casual news viewers interested in tomorrow's forecast no longer needed to stay up to watch, news viewership has stabilized and broadcasters are leveraging the investment in their news departments to create more hours of programming in lieu of syndicated options. Moreover, with the local newspapers continuing to cut staff and fill their pages with wire services, local TV news is becoming firmly established as the primary source of information on breaking news, severe weather, local sports coverage, political coverage and investigative journalism.

From a content perspective, local television stations function as a producer of owned content, a licensee of syndicated content and a franchise affiliate for network content. From a distribution perspective, local television is again a middleman, selling their owned content and reselling their network's content to the MVPDs (cable and satellite distributors) who own the customer relationship. Retrans fees from MVPDs represent as much as 25 percent of revenue and growing.

Retransmission fees are an important new revenue stream for local broadcasters, but are also being coveted by the networks to help subsidize rising content costs including sports rights and original programming. Most stations are protected under long-term affiliate contracts, but as leverage shifts to the networks and OTT distribution platforms become mainstream, either DTC apps offered by the networks or OTT bundles which include their programming could substantially alter relationships with local affiliates. Local television affiliates are already experiencing demands for a higher share of retrans fees while the networks are diluting the exclusivity of the content they provide by expanding distribution on OTT digital video platforms or through DTC apps.

Though their principal distribution is through MVPDs, local TV stations continue to broadcast their signals across their designated coverage areas to fill in gaps created by cord-cutters and people who have never subscribed—also known as "cord-nevers." As the traditional pay TV ecosystem slowly contracts, the broadcast spectrum highly coveted by mobile carriers to fortify network capacity in order to meet the rising demand for online video is also becoming more important to broadcasters as they look to distribute their content to Millennials demanding a free, over-the-air alternative.

The monetization analysis is also mixed. Viewership will continue to decline due to a combination of pay TV subscriber declines, availability of network programming on digital platforms and greater audience fragmentation. Advertising rates will also continue to be under pressure due to increased supply of online video impressions and improved ad technology optimizing price and targeting.

The combined effect of fewer ratings points and weakening pricing leverage will conspire to create a challenging environment for local television's ad revenue stream. Conversely, the gross retrans revenue stream will continue to grow as rate increases will outpace sub losses in the near term, but the exigent risk will be the network's demands for reverse comp and their increased negotiating leverage when the affiliate agreements expire.

Local broadcast television is clearly in transition with both revenue streams under long-term pressure and their most important content suppliers gaining leverage in retrans/reverse comp negotiations with a credible threat to bypass the affiliate network altogether by becoming a linear cable network as well as distributing direct to consumer through OTT bundles and single DTC apps.

The consolidation trend in the industry is a positive development to help increase leverage with both the networks and the pay TV distributors. This strategy can provide a useful delay for the potential bypass strategy by the networks. Scale through consolidation will also help broadcast television groups to invest in programming and begin to recast themselves more in the image of the networks themselves with high quality content they can amortize across a larger platform. A second tier of quasi-national networks could emerge over the next decade, spawned by the need for premium content to complement local news product as they compete for viewership to drive ad revenue and to help command higher fees per subscriber from local video distributors.

Local TV is facing increased competition on all fronts. Its strongest asset is news content so TV stations will likely become more local as they seek to differentiate themselves from the massive amounts of video content being created and distributed online. They will continue to expand news programming including local sports.

It's likely that station owners will also continue to consolidate to gain scale and leverage with broadcast networks, content distributors, syndicators and producers. Advertising will continue to be a challenged revenue stream and broadcasters will generate more online video to increase impressions to mitigate falling ad rates. Another benefit of more locally originated programming is more owned inventory throughout the day to take to market. Though the FCC declined to provide ownership relief in the 2014 Quadrennial Review, it's possible that it will be revisited in 2018 under a new administration. Lifting national ownership caps and relaxing cross-ownership rules to allow intra-market consolidation will be essential regulatory accommodations to preserve the voice and community service of local broadcasters over the long term.

Distribution is upside for local TV as a source of cash derived through current and future spectrum auctions. There will also be an increased reliance on broadcast signals as pay TV subs continue to decline and new, easy-to-use accessories come to market enabling televisions to receive digital broadcast signals. Broadcasters are also working on a new transmission standard (ATSC 3.0) that will provide for interactivity. It would take years to develop, test and rollout, but it is a long-term plus for the spectrum holders.

In addition, TV stations will experiment with more ways to monetize exclusive content through new OTT bundles, DTC consumer apps and digital online video impressions. Moreover, improved data from set-top boxes and OTT platforms distributing local TV content will enable broadcasters to serve addressable and even interactive ads. This is potentially a game changer for local television to help them remain relevant to marketers, offsetting some of the expected CPM erosion due to increased supply of digital video impressions.

BROADCAST NETWORKS

The basic content model of broadcast networks (ABC, CBS, FOX and NBC) has remained extremely consistent. The four network's formats are all similar, in part due to the need to accommodate the local affiliate base. They all have evening news, morning news programs, Sunday morning news programs, live professional and collegiate sports, prime time scripted dramas, reality programming, situational comedies and late night variety shows. The network formats evolved out of the 1960s, '70s and early '80s when they were the only viable choice prior to the introduction of cable. Cable networks were launched in the 1980s and '90s with more focused or niche formats similar to radio stations and as a result, viewership flipped over the last 20 years from 70/30 in favor of broadcasters to 30/70 in favor of the cable networks in the multichannel pay TV ecosystem.

Network ratings continue to reflect increasing fragmentation as Millennials and Generation Xers consume more video online and to a lesser extent, as they delay household formation and avoid the high cost of a pay television or find cheaper alternatives.

Broadcast networks find themselves in a Catch 22-type situation as they seek to defend cash flow. Advertising which makes up approximately 85 percent of their revenue is at the early stages of a long secular decline due to shift of advertising to digital, and more specifically, to online video.

The networks are also in a perpetual negotiation with their affiliates for an increased share of the retransmission fees the broadcasters receive from the pay TV distributors for the right to carry their signals. Revenue is certainly a challenge, but so are costs. Sports rights continue to escalate, but remain the primary draw for viewers and provide the greatest leverage over the affiliates on retrans fee sharing (reverse comp) because the content is viewed as indispensable. Non-sports content costs are rising as well due to the number of new SVOD (subscription video on demand) services in the marketplace beginning with Netflix, Amazon and Hulu, who are all producing original content and bidding for existing product.

Distribution, however, is a potential strategic lever for the broadcast networks. They could bypass the affiliate structure and become a premium cable channel arguably commanding the highest tier of fees. For context, ESPN's roughly $80 annual fee per subscriber is greater than that of all the local broadcast retransmission fees combined. Putting this in perspective, the network affiliates each have stronger ratings than ESPN sign-on to sign-off with the exception of Monday Night football, which is ESPN's highest, rated program. By way of comparison, however, Sunday Night Football on NBC generally draws twice the audience of Monday Night Football on ESPN. The broadcast networks remain the premium content destinations that continue to draw the largest audiences with must-see programming which serves as a unique promotional platform to drive both audience flow and appointment viewing.

As affiliate deals expire, networks could move to control their distribution directly with the consumer—a radical departure from the current structure where they distribute to affiliates who then redistribute to the pay TV distributors (MVPDs) who ultimately own the customer relationship.

Networks could go direct to consumer like CBS has done with a dedicated app. They can also offer their content in over-the-top (OTT) bundles on a non-exclusive basis becoming part of OTT "skinny" bundles that are essentially subscription video on demand (SVOD) services like Sling TV, Netflix or ad-supported video on demand (AVOD) services like Hulu. Consumers value commercial-free video experiences and would likely respond favorably to an SVOD offering at the right price point and if the user experience was highly intuitive and premised on the 4 C's of connectivity, convenience, choice and cost.

The length and staggered expirations of the affiliate agreements coupled with growth of retrans fees from affiliates all but ensure that a strategic imperative to control all IP content distribution and own the customer relationship will play out over a decade or more. The more probable outcome will see networks exerting leverage where they can which means that affiliates will likely be an easier target from which to find value than the NFL.

Importantly, advertiser demand for network content remains healthy. The large and unique audiences viewing mostly in real time are still highly valued by marketers and will continue to drive the imbalance between consumers' time spent with online video versus its decidedly smaller share of ad dollars. The broadcast network's probable strategy of continuing to distribute through the traditional pay TV ecosystem will also serve as a governor on the shift of television ad spend to digital video. Moreover, each of the big four broadcast networks have significant owned and operated (O&O) television station groups which would be disadvantaged in any type of OTT-only strategy that bypasses the traditional affiliate base. Ultimately the disparate asset mixes of each network's parent company will determine their priorities and dictate their competitive strategy.

CABLE NETWORKS

The average person watches about 18 channels per month, but there are over 10 times that many in the traditional pay TV bundle. The number of cable networks has exploded in the last 20 years as the pay TV ecosystem looked unassailable and MVPDs were able to raise costs with impunity. In a study published by the FCC, pay television rates increased an average of 6.1 percent per year from 1995-2013, which was four times the rate of inflation during that period. With subscriber numbers peaking in 2010 and local broadcasters and their network content partners negotiating aggressively for share of the roughly $100 billion pay TV subscriber revenue, cable nets have a series of challenges facing them.

The term "indispensable" has often been used by the most powerful networks when negotiating carriage agreements, but now they are being viewed through a different lens. MVPDs are looking aggressively to project operating margins and scrutinizing all renewals or new channel proposals through a much more discerning filter that ties projected sub losses to the renewal discussions of a channel. This is compelling cable networks to spend more on content and marketing to drive ratings and promote their relevance in the pay TV bundle as carriage renewals with escalators are no longer a given.

Content costs are rising for cable networks just as they are for the broadcast nets. Sports rights have seen dramatic increases which have had significant operational impact on Turner's TNT and Disney's ESPN with both networks having to resort to lay-offs in an ongoing effort to trim operating costs to mitigate the impact of the new sports rights deals as well as lower ad revenues due to the overall fragmentation of video exacerbated by cord-cutting Millennials and a surfeit of online video impressions.

ESPN and TNT are arguably the two most valuable cable networks respectively earning approximately $80 and $20 annually per sub and they are both having a difficult time generating growth in operating income due to escalating content costs and slowing revenue growth as both revenue streams—subscriber and advertising—are facing headwinds. The cost of producing a television series is also rising because of the competition for actors, writers and directors driven by new OTT players like Netflix and Amazon as well as existing cable and broadcast nets spending on content to remain competitive and relevant.

From a distribution perspective, most cable networks won't have the leverage to separate their digital streaming rights from their carriage agreements and the distributors don't want to lose exclusivity to digital platforms, which only encourage more subscriber defections.

The MVPDs will be pushing for distribution on digital platforms through the "TV Everywhere" approach that authenticates viewers with pay TV subscriptions to distribute content to mobile devices. Powerful networks like TNT, USA, CBS, FX, Showtime and HBO will employ digital distribution for new consumer offerings to provide a unique and powerful user experience that they can't currently offer on linear cable.

With binge-viewing becoming a behavioral norm, the cable networks will want to allow all episodes previously aired from the current season to be available on demand through their streaming apps and also through cable on demand in order to build audiences by allowing viewers to catch up.

As the content model evolves, networks will want access to the current season of television shows known as "stacking," which allows the networks to offer entire seasons at once rather than episodically throughout the season. They also want the ability to offer past seasons which they believe will help build fan bases and loyal audiences, putting cable nets at odds with studios. The basic model of a studio maximizes the revenue for a given piece of content by selling it to multiple buyers, each with rights to air it in specific periods of time or windows. This would be in conflict with a network's DTC app that offered unfettered access to both the current and past seasons of a show thus obviating the studio's ability to window it.

The monetization model for cable nets is getting squeezed from lower advertising rates and subscriber losses. With Millennials watching less traditional TV due to their increased consumption of online video, the coveted 18-49 demographic is showing multi-year declines for most cable television networks.

The 18-49 year-olds—particularly the younger Millennials—are disconnecting from the traditional pay TV ecosystem and spending their time with SVOD offerings like Netflix and Amazon, as well as ad-based video on-demand platforms like Hulu and YouTube. Declining ratings, declining ad rates and declining subscribers are all putting stress on the traditional pay television ecosystem. As a result, sub fee negotiations are becoming more contentious as both sides have more at stake with smaller margins for error. Poorly rated channels will be given the choice of lower or even no sub fees or alternatively face non-renewal in the Modern Media ecosystem where the market for content will function more efficiently.

Content and marketing will require more investment to drive awareness, relevancy and ratings. As the traditional pay TV ecosystem continues to contract, there will be a shakeout of mediocre channels to create a more flexible and competitive bundle. Consumers will have the ability to create more bespoke bundles either through their MVPD or by working around them to assemble compelling OTT alternatives to the legacy 180 channel bundle. Over time, many of the non-top tier brands will be relegated to an ad-supported model, which will likely prove to be unsustainable models given their cost structures.

MULTICHANNEL VIDEO PROGRAM DISTRIBUTORS (MVPDS)

MVPDs are distribution businesses that license content from programmers including broadcast and cable networks and resell it to consumers. Cable, satellite and telephone companies each compete to sell packages to consumers including television, telephone, broadband and home security. For the cable and Telco companies, their "pipe" into the home can distribute all of these products reinforcing the power of their subscription business model. The incremental cost of selling broadband to a video customer or voice to a broadband customer is practically zero, so while extremely capital intensive, the MVPDs enjoy excellent operating margins.

The cable companies have had an inherent advantage over the satellite distributors because of the cable pipe's two-way capabilities whereas a satellite delivers content or data with a one-way transmission—satellite to receiver.

The industrial logic behind the AT&T-DirecTV merger was to combine the customer-base of the second largest MVPD with AT&T's fully distributed communications network to create an end-to-end video, voice and data solution for customers. Integrations of this complexity are highly difficult and generally take years to fully realize the strategic vision. If management executes, it will create a more viable competitor to the incumbent cable distributor in every market. In the near term, the incumbent cable companies are best positioned to leverage their technology, infrastructure and customer relationships to compete simultaneously in the traditional pay TV ecosystem while innovating the business model to leverage their broadband capabilities in the emerging digital video distribution business.

MVPDs spend approximately $500 annually per subscriber on video content distributed among over 150 different channels. The challenge for distributors is to find ways to trim the bundle without consumers perceiving a loss of value. The cord-cutting and cord-never phenomenon have as much to do with price as technology. Millennials have wider interests and a plethora of alternatives for video-based entertainment. MVPDs are at a point of inflection with a bifurcated customer base, so they will need to evolve from a "one size fits all" pricing model to appeal to a digitally-oriented generation who are aggressively looking for more cost efficient alternatives. Fortunately for the MVPDs, it's also one of the few business models in media where the incumbent is also the disruptor.

In other words, the next generation distribution channel for video is Internet Protocol (IP) distributed over the high-speed broadband that cable and telephone companies are already selling consumers and businesses for voice and data. Speed, reliability, price and customer service are the operative dimensions on which network distributors compete and the incumbent MVPDs will likely have an edge in all of these areas against a new entrant who tries to compete at scale.

With approximately only 5 percent of revenue coming from advertising sales, the monetization model is subscription-based and with the eventual transition to IP video through smaller and more bespoke bundles, the key to revenue growth will be to minimize churn and sell more products to the existing customer base. The MVPDs revenue mix will shift over time, but the model is sound as consumer and enterprise demand for more robust broadband networks will be a constant for years to come.

ONLINE VIDEO

The online video space is experiencing the same growth cycle as ad technology. A wide range of disparate start-ups led by entrepreneurs who wake up every day focused on disrupting the incumbents like television programmers and distributors or in the case of ad tech, the agency complex that plans and buys media. Online video offers several key points of differentiation from the traditional television ecosystem including: mobile-centric, vast content libraries, on-demand content, smaller bundles, user-generated content, smarter impressions, flexible formats for content and advertising tailored to individuals and optimized for devices. The amount of video content being created on a daily basis is staggering with YouTube reporting 300 hours of new content being uploaded every minute, which translates into 49 years of continuous video being uploaded every day to YouTube alone, not to mention Facebook, Snapchat, Twitter and dozens of other scaled digital platforms distributing live and on-demand video.

Multichannel Networks (MCNs) are looking to create distribution-centric business models similar to the models pioneered by record labels as they trolled the clubs for garage bands with hit potential. MCNs employ a high-tech A&R strategy of mining the web for videos with true viral potential and signing talent before their potential is obvious. Similar to labels, it's an aggregation play to build a stable of talent, provide marketing and production support necessary to build a loyal fan base. Some of these branded "channels" will have subscription potential, but most will be part of the ad-supported ecosystem of video on demand (AVOD).

These AVOD platforms are also serving as an advertising laboratory of sorts where new formats for native and interactive advertising are being tested and refined, leveraging the marketing power of the new crop of digital media stars. The global reach of online video enables emerging stars to be discovered and commercialized in a matter of months as opposed to years under the inherent constraints of the traditional ecosystem. The multiplatform monetization potential of entertainers and influencers known as YouTube "sensations" includes ad-supported through sponsored-content as well as subscription media, live events and licensing.

OTT video offerings feature more traditional television content distributed digitally and on demand. OTT refers to coming over the top of the traditional pay TV ecosystem which consists primarily of linear cable networks and an increasing amount of on-demand content offered by the MVPD.

Consumers prefer the convenience of on-demand content over a linear alternative where they have to make the effort to DVR content they wish to view at a later time. Think of OTT offerings as a digital video content distribution business that operates over the legacy cable company's broadband network as their distribution platform. OTT distributors like Netflix, Amazon, Hulu, YouTube and Facebook can compete with the likes of Comcast for video subscriptions using the cable company's own broadband network as a free distribution channel to establish an independent customer relationship on top of the broadband provider's relationship.

Liberated from the capital requirements to build and maintain a broadband network, OTT digital video distributors can invest in exclusive content and customer acquisition. Individual networks will also come to market as OTT apps using the promotional power of their legacy, linear platforms to market directly to their viewers. The offerings will likely evolve to be a subscription product through an app, which offers linear as well as on-demand content featuring both commerce and interactive opportunities. The DTC apps will also be bundled by OTT distributors to, in effect, recreate a smaller, personalized cable bundle that offers the consumer a more user-friendly and entertaining viewing experience.

The OTT distribution model is creating a hyper competitive marketplace for exclusive content, which is likely to include live sports as league contracts come up for renewal in the next decade. As the bundle becomes more bespoke and the differentiated offerings with exclusive content become more plentiful, the $100 billion that consumers currently pay for video subscriptions is likely to begin growing again at an attractive rate, materially reshaping the pay TV ecosystem by 2025.

LOCAL BROADCAST RADIO

Broadcast radio is best summed up by Mark Twain's famous quote: "The reports of my death have been greatly exaggerated." The digital pundits have been predicting the demise of America's first electronic mass medium for over 20 years, but the facts tell a different story. According to Nielsen's Total Audience Survey, more than 90 percent of all adults listen to the radio each week, compared with 87 percent of adults who watch TV in a given week making broadcast radio America's number one reach medium.

Adults listen more than two hours per day, principally in the automobile. Radio's distribution model is free, over-the-air and ad-supported. There are over 270 million cars and trucks on the road and virtually all of them have radio, which for most consumers is easier to use than a toaster. The terrestrial radio broadcast distribution system is one of best in the world for coverage and spectrum integrity and like broadcast TV, the vast majority of radio stations broadcast digital audio using an industry standard known as HD radio. Radio's distribution and situational usage are unique among media because it generally reaches consumers in their car while they are a captive audience. In other words, they are not engaged with multiple screens texting, on social media, watching videos, playing games or shopping while driving with the radio on.

Radio offers advertisers the opportunity to have an intimate, focused conversation with consumers. Since there is only an average of approximately 1.2 persons per vehicle in town and 1.5 on the highway, radio functions as the trusted companion and principal source of information and entertainment while in the car.

Radio content is primarily local and serves as a valuable medium to keep consumers connected while driving around town to work, school, restaurants, activities, entertainment, shopping, errands and appointments. Consumers tend to listen to the same stations and develop "listener" relationships with on-air personalities over a period of years listening to them as part of their daily routine while in the car or waking up and getting their day started.

Radio content tends to be presented in focused offerings around branded channels, similar to cable networks. News, sports and political talk along with genre-specific stations like Country, Top 40, R&B, Oldies, Rock, Hip Hop and many others are available across the country, free of charge, supported by advertising. Also, because of its leading reach, radio continues to be the most popular way people discover new music. Radio programmers have been working in tandem with the labels for decades to create superstar artists and bands by breaking music and exposing it with enough frequency or "spins" to introduce a new sound to the masses. Radio serves as a curator and promoter to the record labels while creating entertaining and informative content through local on-air talent, which differentiates stations and builds loyal audiences.

Radio broadcasters are also in the enviable position of owning both their content and distribution, and in a key difference with TV broadcasters, more than 95 percent of radio listening occurs through the terrestrial broadcast signal. The value proposition to the consumer remains strong as a free, convenient, entertaining, informative and local companion in the car. Radio has protected distribution, limiting broadcast competition through the FCC and enjoys the lowest content rights fees in the music business. Radio's content and distribution both have comparative strengths against most other media models.

Radio's biggest challenge is monetization because it's essentially 100 percent ad-supported and therefore subject to the vicissitudes of the ad market. Moreover, like TV, it's a fixed inventory business, so downward pressure on ad rates due to a surfeit of supply can't be overcome with increased volume.

Radio is also a high fixed-cost business, so declining revenue is difficult to offset through ongoing cost reductions. As a one-to-many medium, radio is mass-targeted through its different formats, but cannot offer individual addressability through its broadcast channel.

The way forward for radio broadcasters is to leverage the market leading reach to create multiplatform brands with additional revenue streams. Radio needs to expand its vision of the customer relationship, which it owns as the last mile distributor. Radio has a unique relationship and loyal bond with listeners, which can be leveraged into an expanded business model including subscription-based audio on-demand, live streaming audio and video, live and recorded entertainment, themed events and digital commerce. Further industry consolidation will help drive scale efficiencies and leverage with key vendors. Radio's reach and listener loyalty give it viability, but the business model has to evolve to create more advertising and sponsorship opportunities as well as a share of the listener's entertainment dollar.

SATELLITE RADIO

SiriusXM is arguably one of the best business models in all of media. The satellite radio company is a subscription-based, premium audio service that is vertically integrated, producing content and distributing it through a proprietary network. In addition to subscriber revenue, SiriusXM also monetizes its spoken word content through its own sales force and owns the customer relationships for its 30+ million subscribers.

It's also the only satellite delivered, premium audio service resulting from a merger of the only two licensed competitors. Monopolies are generally good businesses and this happens to be a great one and there is more upside in monetization. Over 80 million cars have an inactive receiver so each 1 percent conversion creates roughly $100 million of revenue, which flows through the income statement at a very high conversion rate to operating profit. The potential downside for the premium audio subscription service is competition in the "connected car" from wireless broadband.

Apple and Google are aggressively working to make iOS and Android the operating systems in car, or put another way, make the car dashboard an extension of either the iPhone or Android device depending upon which device is connected. As cars become connected extensions of smartphones, a slew of offerings—similar to OTT video—will come to market for subscription audio likely including local stations offered commercial-free which will represent the first true non-broadcast radio competition for SiriusXM in the car.

It can preserve its subscription dominance in the car by disrupting itself through digital streaming and on-demand audio content offerings at different price points to appeal to listeners who choose to power their car's entertainment experience through their phone. They could also explore possible tie-ups with large broadcast groups and digital pure plays for content, promotion, mobile distribution and ad sales infrastructure.

Partnering with broadcast radio with locally addressable channels could give top local talent an additional venue to create content away from the linear broadcast channel similar to SiriusXM's Howard Stern Channel. Conversely, fledgling brands like the Highway country music channel on SiriusXM can also be extended to broadcast and internet radio as part of a larger strategy to build multiplatform brands.

The power of the subscription model drives the economics of the strategy to secure incremental subs in key large, local markets that are passionate fans of local talent and serves as one of the more surefire ways of reactivating existing vehicles.

INTERNET RADIO

Streaming audio, also known as internet radio, is divided into pure play streamers like Pandora, which stream music playlists curated by the service and pushed to the consumer, and distributors of traditional radio content via live digital stream or original content through on-demand podcasts—all delivered through apps. iHeart and TuneIn are the largest aggregators and redistributors of local broadcast radio content. NPR, along with hundreds of digital distributors, also produce or distribute third-party content on ad-based platforms.

Pandora's user base is 95 percent free, ad-supported as are most all of the internet radio businesses. The model for internet radio is still nascent though the service has been in existence for over a decade. With 80 percent of radio consumption going to traditional broadcasters, internet radio is relegated to just 12 percent of radio listening and its growth rate has slowed.

Though internet radio has better targeting attributes due to addressability and data, the relative reach is far too small to serve as a viable substitute for traditional radio for most advertisers both local and national. Rights fees are also problematic for streamers at 17 cents for every 100 songs streamed, it alone represents more than 50 percent of revenue, which makes for low operating leverage and a challenging business model. Pandora, launched in 2004, and has used their first-mover advantage to dominate the internet radio space with over 80 million active users and over $1 billion of advertising revenue, more than all of its internet radio competitors combined.

Largely unprofitable, internet radio companies are beginning to face growing challenges because they are low margin, ad-based digital distribution businesses that sell an undifferentiated product with low barriers to entry. It's an inviting target for key strategic competitors like Apple, Google and Amazon to aggressively compete for users in both on-demand and playlist services. Internet radio will also face increasing competition in spoken-word content from broadcasters looking to create new revenue streams as well as SiriusXM as they likely expand their digital product offerings as the transition occurs over time to the connected car.

Similar to television, radio has been disrupted by online services, but over time a rationalization will occur and radio, like television, will be seamlessly distributed across analog (broadcast), digital satellite and IP platforms. In other words, consumers won't consider "internet" radio as an alternative to "broadcast" radio because the experience will be undifferentiated for the core linear product. The emerging Modern Media trend will be *pan-audio* brands, which are distributed across multiple platforms.

A host of new, on-demand options when accessing the content through the mobile app will provide an added dimension for users. Incumbent internet radio companies will also expand their content offerings beyond playlists in an effort to grow users and listening hours. If they fail to innovate, new entrants and new offerings by legacy competitors will reshape the digital audio playing field, putting pressure on the business models of the leading digital distributors of ad-based, music playlists like Pandora.

RECORDED MUSIC

The record labels are in the unenviable position of selling a product that is being consumed at all-time levels, yet revenues are down 50 percent from peak. This is mostly due to piracy and legitimate services, which are free to the consumer and supported by advertising. People love music and are listening to it more than ever due to the convenience and mass adoption of mobile devices, but the existential threat to the music industry is that consumers no longer value content as they did in the 1990s pre-Napster era. Consumers' perceived value of music is declining and is being exacerbated by the label's second problem after piracy, which is an abundance of free product.

Beginning with iTunes and now including free, on-demand services like Spotify and YouTube, consumers can legally access free premium music on demand. The same perceived devaluation of content has occurred with journalism due to the widespread availability of premium content, but the same cannot be said for video due to much stricter anti-piracy and copyright enforcement.

Labels controlled their distribution when it was sold as a physical medium, but controlling digital distribution has been elusive and the free services have trained a generation of Millennials that they don't have to pay for music. Labels need to systematically attack both issues to preserve the viability of their industry or it will be increasingly difficult to show growth even though demand for their product is strong. Ultimately, the profitability of the industry will depend upon the size of the addressable market of consumers who believe in the intrinsic value of music content and are willing to foot the bill for a $100 annual music subscription.

Record labels had much greater control of their consumer distribution channel when their product was distributed as a physical medium through retail, because they controlled both the consumer offering (album) as well as the wholesale pricing to retailers. Moreover, the physical medium contained artwork, liner notes and lyrics which created true fan engagement with the artists, which is a key purchase criterion for a significant percentage of music consumers. The mobile revolution, however, has replaced this consumer experience with online streaming, embraced by consumers as a more convenient way to consume content.

Importantly, the bundle (album) was disaggregated allowing consumers to purchase music more efficiently on a song-by-song basis through iTunes. Apple became the dominant retailer of music, which initially held promise for the labels if volume continued to grow, but the iTunes ecosystem was then disrupted by the free on-demand streamers like YouTube and Spotify and a host of internet radio options like Pandora.

The second seminal shift from digital ownership through iTunes to online access through streaming services has completely upended the labels longstanding and highly profitable distribution model, transferring significant value away from the labels as revenue suffered steep declines due to the new digital distributors including YouTube, Spotify, Deezer and Pandora.

The business model of recorded music is transitioning from consumers predictably purchasing music through a tightly controlled retail channel (pre-iTunes) to a model where the product is essentially available for free through on-demand streaming services or alternatively, for purchase on a song-by-song basis. According to the RIAA, in the U.S., digital music downloads and streaming services accounted for more than 70 percent of revenues with physical sales (CDs and vinyl) now accounting for less than 25 percent of sales and continuing to steadily decline. Digital downloads account for approximately 40 percent of revenue and are also declining at roughly the same rate as physical copy sales as consumers continue to abandon both, opting for the free, on-demand services from Spotify, YouTube and Vevo. These free, ad-based, on-demand services are responsible for the majority of digital traffic, but account for only about 12 percent of revenue through rev shares from ad sales.

Subscription services are growing nicely, but are similar in size to the ad revenue generated from the streamers at less than 15 percent of total industry revenue. On its present path, the music industry is slowly transitioning into primarily an ad-supported model with revenue growth relying on increasing the number of ad impressions in a market already burdened with oversupply.

Regaining control over distribution and phasing out free, on-demand access is a strategic imperative to reverse the revenue declines and start to generate real paying subscribers as opposed to the low-yield from bundled wireless carrier deals. The inexorable shift to online, mobile-centric media has created near-term chaos for the labels, but the long-term path to profitability lies in embracing technology and restructuring their distribution channels to reflect their leverage as content providers on behalf of the artists, while they still control the artist, and producer end of the value chain. Recent moves by artists Taylor Swift and Adele to keep their music off free on-demand services are harbingers of the creative community's unrest over declining revenues and could lead to a direct-to-consumer movement by name-brand talent in the absence of a more commercially viable distribution system.

NEWSPAPERS

It's a similar tale to the music industry in which publishers controlled distribution when newspapers were exclusively a physical medium. The shift to digital led to rampant copyright infringement and unauthorized redistribution of content, which created yet another value shift to digital middlemen. This happened because the publishers, like the record companies, didn't act aggressively enough at the outset to control unauthorized distribution through copyright enforcement as well as proactively erecting paywalls.

Consequently, the newspaper business ceded its distribution to a long tail of online distributors who either pirate their content or distribute it free to the consumer, and are supported by advertising, which is then shared with the publisher. Again, similar to music, physical distribution continues to decline with corresponding print advertising off almost 65 percent over a 10-year period from 2005 to 2014 according to Pew. Consumers have also evolved their value perception of online news due to the widespread availability of free content. Paywalls with the exception of the Wall Street Journal, the New York Times and the Financial Times have not gained traction and represent a small fraction of overall industry revenue.

For example, the New York Times has over one million digital subscribers, generating more than $200 million or 15 percent of their total revenue. This is followed by the Wall Street Journal with just under a million subscribers and approximately $175 million per year, followed by a precipitous drop to the Boston Globe and Los Angeles Times, each with about 65,000 subscribers generating only about $15 million in revenue. At 15 percent or less of revenue—identical to what it represents for the music industry—the subscription model for digital newspaper distribution monetizes the content at an unsustainable level which is again, ironically similar to the new economics of recorded music.

The newspaper industry's answer to consumer's rejection of paywalls is to distribute their content as widely as possible, which is should be viewed as a

Faustian bargain. It's a strategy that will irreversibly convert newspapers into disaggregated content producers distributing their articles through third-party apps like Facebook Instant Articles, Google, Twitter and a host of other messaging apps and digital news sites in return for a share of ad revenue while their brands are slowly diluted.

Expect newspapers to continue to experience a double-digit decline in high-margin print advertising and a single-digit decline in print copy sales putting further pressure on fixed costs, most notably the newsrooms. Local television stations will also be competing aggressively for local news ad dollars as they continue to leverage their news departments to create more robust digital offerings and use their ubiquitous market reach to promote and drive traffic to their apps and sites.

Newspapers are fighting for relevancy by evolving their legacy models to aggressively reduce costs while many are also producing more contemporary content to appeal to the younger audiences coveted by marketers. The stand-alone model of the local newspaper is likely to prove unsustainable going into the next decade and will compel in-market consolidation or partnerships with existing local news media including radio or television broadcasters. Distribution will continue to shift to digital with physical copies contracting in both circulation base and frequency of days published as daily newspapers look to find a viable model with no assurances that they will be successful.

MAGAZINES

With the exception of general interest newsweekly publications, magazines have historically served targeted communities of interest. They could appeal to large and diverse communities around sports, fashion, beauty, travel and food or serve much more focused communities like cigar smokers, watch collectors, software developers or HR professionals through trade publications. There are over 7,000 magazines in the U.S. competing for approximately $15 billion in ad revenue and taking in a similar amount in combined subscription revenue and newsstand sales. Newsstand sales, which are essentially impulse buys, make up less than 10 percent of sales and are falling low double digits while ad revenue is declining low single digits. Digital subscriptions and online ad revenues are each growing nicely in excess of 20 percent, but from a comparatively low base. Interestingly, the print subscriber numbers are faring better than newsstand sales due mostly to heavy promotional activity, but not growing.

Aside from weekly newsmagazine, which have been severely challenged by the immediacy of the digital news cycle, magazine content fills a niche with information and analysis on subject areas to specific communities of interest. Successful publications consistently create content that is relevant and unique to their target community.

Moreover, the physical magazines in consumers' homes represent a lifestyle mosaic of sorts as it speaks to their persona. People don't generally display and collect newspapers, but they often do with magazines. The luxury segment is the most poignant example of consumer self-expression where glossy luxury publications become table art and are coveted by luxury advertisers who want to control the context of their message in a sea of digital impressions with much less control over the context in which they are served.

In addition to newsweekly publications, digital distribution has also disproportionately impacted news and celebrity gossip magazines. This is the type of content that is most readily available on the internet with no shortage of celebrity photos and gossip on dozens of popular sites as it drives traffic, page views and ad revenues.

Magazines, like radio stations, that target homogenous communities of interest are best positioned to evolve into multiplatform brands including digital video, podcasts and news distributed through mobile apps, as well as live events and commerce. This opportunity applies for both consumer and trade publications. A common prescription for all ad-based businesses is to create more inventory and stronger consumer engagement through an integrated multiplatform strategy as well as diversification into commerce through live events and premium subscription offerings.

Magazines have a unique opportunity to reinvent their business models because of their market knowledge, which will play a key role in the future of media enabling publishers to super-serve well-defined communities of interest. It will be imperative to invest in content that lives outside of the printed page to create more touch points throughout the day and week with their communities of interest. The publication is a credible foundation on which to build a multiplatform franchise brand with diversified revenue streams and occupy a meaningful position in the new Modern Media landscape.

CONCLUSION

Legacy media companies are very much in control of their destiny as they own trusted brands, vast libraries of popular content and most importantly, have the domain knowledge and experience to consistently produce premium content in hit-driven businesses. These legacy companies are also very much in a transitional phase as they grapple with the five key themes driving the paradigm shift to modern media. Over time, they will cede their analog distribution platforms like DVDs, newspapers, CDs and magazines, and longer term, this will also include linear TV channels migrating to IP video and on-demand distribution.

Premium content in the traditional forms of television, radio, music, movies, journalism, magazines and games will continue to enjoy robust consumer demand while innovative new formats will emerge to keep content relevant and engaging for future generations of consumers. Content creators will innovate on a larger canvas as distribution inexorably shifts to IP platforms and content is liberated from legacy formats.

Technology companies will increasingly serve as vendors, partners, competitors and even acquirers of traditional media companies as the digital and traditional media ecosystems continue to converge. New business models will emerge around subscription-based, personalized media leveraging IoT technology to create unimaginable levels of personalization for both content and advertising. Legacy business models, particularly around analog distribution and traditional ad sales, will continue to be disrupted by the shift to mobile platforms compelling further consolidation across the continuum from publishers to marketers.

The vision for "The New Modern Media" is in clear focus and the inevitable journey will create boundless opportunities for those who take part in building the future.

ACKNOWLEDGEMENTS

My brothers David, John and Michael as we've worked together to build media companies over the last 25 years.

My good friend Drew Marcus, an investor and distinguished media analyst, for being a thoughtful and constructive sounding board as I developed the vision and frameworks for The New Modern Media.

I also want to thank Sean Bertram at Tourbillon International for his focus and dedication throughout the intricate publishing process to bring this project to fruition and to his colleague, Gregory Odendahl for his creativity on the cover design and interior layout.

Lastly, I'd like to thank my wife and muse, Vanessa, for her patience and support as I spent the better part of a year writing this book.

GLOSSARY OF TERMS

Ad Exchange — a technology platform that facilitates the buying and selling of media advertising inventory from multiple ad networks. Prices for the inventory are generally determined through bidding. The approach is technology-driven and serves to make an efficient market between marketers and publishers.

Addressable Users — the ability to single-out or "address" individual users through one-to-one IP-based distribution as opposed to the non-addressable nature of one-to-many broadcast distribution. Addressability enables content publishers and marketers alike to serve individualized content for a more personalized user experience.

Ad Tech — a general term for a category of services which connect marketers to publishers including: demand-side platforms, data management platforms, supply-side platforms, ad servers, ad networks, ad exchanges, real-time bidding, yield optimization, data optimization and creative optimization.

Analog — the literal definition is something measurable by a continuously variable physical quantity such as spatial position or voltage. In media, it refers to legacy or non-digital media such as: newspapers, magazines, broadcast television, linear cable network and broadcast or satellite radio. Analog media is linear and/or is distributed through a physical medium.

App — short for application software program and most generally refers to programs designed to run on mobile devices. If the app is native, it runs directly on the mobile device rather than though the mobile browser

AQH — an acronym that stands for Average Quarter Hour and is a measurement unit used by Nielsen to estimate the number of people watching or listening to TV or radio in any given 15-minute period of time. It is generally expressed as either AQH Persons, which estimates the number of people listening in an average quarter hour; AQH Share, which estimates the share of available audience viewing or listening in a given time period, or AQH Rating, which estimates the number of viewers or listeners out of the entire sample universe, not just the people consuming media at that time.

A&R — stands for Artist & Repertoire, which is a functional department of record labels and music publishing companies. A&R professionals are charged with discovering and developing talent including recording artists, songwriters, musicians and producers.

AVOD — Advertising Video On Demand. YouTube is the most popular AVOD service.

Bit — It's short for binary digit. A bit is the fundamental or base unit of information in computing and digital communications. A bit is binary and thus can have only one of two values, which are most commonly expressed as 0 or 1.

Bot — an automated application that executes specific tasks over the internet usually at a very high speed making them popular for labor intensive and repetitive activities.

Bundle — the package of television channels typically offered in pay subscription from MVPDs including cable, satellite and telco. OTT (Over-the-Top) digital distributors also offer bundles, which are generally smaller and more customized known as Skinny Bundles.

Cloud — a shared pool of internet-based computing resources housed in large data centers, which contain both applications and data. Users can access these resources on demand through the internet and they can be updated centrally in real time for improved efficiency.

Cookies — data sent from websites to a user's browser, which reports back on user behavior within the site and maintains a history for the publisher. Cookies can also follow a user on other sites for the purpose of serving them "retargeted" ads. They can also remember passwords, addresses and credit card information for frequently visited sites.

Content — the fundamental product of media including audio, video, text and images—live or recorded. Also used by media companies to distinguish themselves from companies who simply distribute rather than produce, buy or license content.

Core Data — empirical data prior to having analytics applied against it. It includes: age, gender, marital status, children, income, education, occupation, home ownership, product registration such as cars and consumer electronics.

CPM — Cost Per Thousand. A common metric used in advertising to normalize the cost of reaching a thousand people with a single message or impression.

Curation — a term commonly used in digital media parlance to describe a focused product offering which is selected from a wider range of options to create a more desirable experience for the end-user.

Derivative Data — a set of data which have been analyzed to produce incremental or enhanced insights derived from disparate sets of core data. Using analytics, data scientists can draw conclusions, which in turn inform key decisions regarding content, distribution and monetization.

Digital — unlike analog, digital is virtual or non-spatial. Digital media can be any combination of audio, video, text and images, which can be stored as bits and transmitted on demand.

Distributor — any entity which distributes content as individual pieces such as an individual song on iTunes, through a bundle such as pay television from a cable provider or a newspaper which distributes content through both physical and digital mediums.

DMP — Data Management Platform. A virtual warehouse of data used by marketers to segment audiences and develop targeting strategies for digital marketing campaigns.

Download — commonly refers to transferring content such as songs, movies, television show, books, newspapers and magazines from a server to a device such as a PC, tablet, smartphone or wearable.

DSP — Demand-Side Platform. Enables marketers to manage multiple ad exchanges and execute buys across multiple ad networks with sophisticated targeting, real-time bidding and optimization.

DTC — Direct to Consumer. A distribution channel that media brands are increasingly employing to bypass or supplement traditional distributors like MVPDs. DTC offerings can be either singular or in bundles offered by OTT digital distributors.

Dynamic Advertising — the ability to serve a message that is optimized for content, context and device to an individual. The goal is to serve the right ad to the right prospect at the right time to maximize engagement and activation.

Ecosystem— an interconnected system of media companies which participate in various parts of the value chain including content, distribution and monetization.

eSports — an emerging and rapidly growing spectator sport watching video game players compete against one another live as well as online.

Freemium — a popular business model adopted by digital media companies that employs a customer acquisition strategy where users can experience a service at a basic level for free with the goal of upselling them to an enhanced version for a fee. Freemium models are typically characterized by a small percentage of total users, but accounting for the vast majority of revenue.

Gamer — a term used to describe active enthusiasts of video games.

GRP — Gross Rating Point. A metric used by buyers and sellers of media to indicate the amount of gross impressions including audience duplication in a particular media buy or total campaign.

Impression — a single message that is served to an individual person.

Interactive — a two-way media experience that enables consumers to interact with the content providing a more immersive experience with deeper levels of engagement.

IoT — Internet of Things. Anything with an IP address can be addressed by any connected device. In media, any individual piece of content including songs, books, videos, movies, television shows, articles, magazines and images can be tagged with an IP address and therefore accessible by any connected device to create a truly personalized media experience.

IP — Internet Protocol. A formalized communications protocol or format for sending digital messaging across the internet.

Linear — a media format where content is served serially in real time. Radio and television broadcasting including cable networks and satellite radio are all examples of linear media.

Marketer — also known as "advertiser." Marketers sell products to consumers and use media to help facilitate and execute their communications strategies.

MCN — Multichannel Network. MCNs are digital media companies, which identify, produce, distribute, market and monetize aspiring and emerging talent through digital media.

Media Mix — the portfolio of media buys used by marketers to execute a campaign.

Medium — legacy media platforms and distribution channels including radio, television, newspaper, magazine, books, CDs, DVDs and digital devices, which serve as distribution channels for content.

Messaging Platform — digital apps which enable users to communicate either one-to-one or one-to-many through text, video, audio and images distributed via the internet.

Mobile — wireless IP distribution to devices such as smartphones and tablets controlled by mobile operating systems including Android and iOS.

Monetization — generating revenue from content indirectly through an ad-supported model or direct to consumer through a subscription or transaction model.

Multiplatform — serving branded content across multiple mediums or platforms including digital, broadcast television and radio, linear cable, satellite, print, live events and commerce.

MVPD — Multiple Video Program Distributor. Used to describe cable, satellite and telco distributors of pay television.

Network Effect — the phenomenon that makes a network more valuable to each individual user with the addition of each incremental user.

Net Neutrality — an FCC policy which mandates that broadband providers treat all traffic on their network equally and without prejudice providing the same speeds for all traffic regardless of affiliation or commercial relationship with the broadband provider.

Nonlinear — opposite of linear where content is distributed on demand and most commonly refers to OTT digital video and streaming audio distributors.

On Demand — a method of distributing content that is stored in the cloud and can be accessed by users at any time on any connected device with proper authentication.

Online — content or services which are distributed over the internet through fixed and wireless (mobile) platforms.

OTT — Over the Top. Digital content distribution via fixed or mobile broadband that is both a substitute and complement for the traditional pay television bundle.

Paywall — a feature on websites and apps which "hides" premium content from non-paying users. Publishers decide how which content belongs on either side of a paywall to maximize traffic, yet create a compelling enough value proposition to drive consumers to subscribe.

Peer-to-peer — a data warehousing site that enables users to upload content which is then stored and subsequently downloaded by "peers." It's a form of file sharing, which is often linked to piracy and copyright infringement.

Producer — a term commonly used for content creators who "produce" audio, video, text and image content.

Programmatic — a form of data-driven, automated ad buying that employs real time bidding (RTB) to secure the most cost efficient impression across media platforms and publishers which meets the stated targeting objectives of the media buy.

Publisher — the content owner, licensee and/or distributor who controls access to their content by consumers and marketers.

Rating Point — a rating point is equal to 1 percent of the total audience. For example, the Super Bowl attracts approximately 120 million viewers out of a total audience of 250 million for a 48 rating or 48 percent of the total audience whether they are watching television during that time or not.

Retargeting — a digital advertising technique that targets individual users as opposed to sites. If you search for a brand of pickup truck, you will likely see ads for that truck brand (or others) on various auto-related sites as well as on sites that are completely unrelated to automobiles.

Retrans Fees — fees paid to local broadcasters by MVPDs for the privilege of distributing their signals to local subscribers.

Reverse Comp — fees paid to broadcast networks by local broadcast affiliates for the privilege of distributing their content and reselling it to the MVPDs.

Rich Media — an internet advertising term for ad products which may include audio and video and offer consumers the ability to engage and interact with the content to provide a higher level of engagement with the brand.

ROI — Return on Investment. A commonly used metric by marketers to determine the sales lift from an advertising campaign against the investment required to achieve it.

Spectrum — short for Electromagnetic Spectrum of which a finite segment is deployed as radio waves for radio and television broadcasting, Wi-Fi and mobile broadband.

SSP — Supply-Side Platform. It's a more sophisticated form of ad network that enables publishers to offer their inventory to the widest possible demand set of marketers. SSPs also enable publishers to compete on multiple ad exchanges with smart impressions to optimize value in real-time auctions.

Stacking — the practice of digital video distributors releasing entire current seasons of a television series to heighten consumer interest by enabling new viewers to catch-up while satisfying the need of a growing consumer segment of "binge viewers."

Streaming — serving IP video or audio either on demand or in real time.

SVOD — Subscription Video On Demand. Digital video distributors which rely on a subscription model to give paying subscribers access to their library of on-demand content. Netflix is the largest SVOD provider.

Targeting — a digital marketing term which employs derivative data to develop sophisticated audience segments for ad buys to maximize ROI.

TVOD — Transaction Video On Demand. Similar to SVOD, TVOD is also pay-for-play with the exception that it d oesn't employ a subscription model, but rather a pay as you go approach most commonly used by MVPDs for movies on demand.

Value Chain — the continuum which includes all of the inputs from content creation through content consumption. This includes production, distribution and monetization and involves dozens of sub-industries and thousands of companies which compete for business at their respective points in the value chain.

VR — Virtual Reality. VR is 21st century computing platform, which creates a unique and totally immersive user experience designed to make the user believe they are transported from their current reality into the context of the VR content. It was first popularized by the aviation and aerospace industries to train pilots and astronauts and is currently being commercialized for the general market.

ABOUT THE AUTHOR

Lew Dickey is an entrepreneur and media executive with over 30 years of industry experience.

In 1996, Dickey conceived a plan to take advantage of the 1996 Telco Act to consolidate the radio market. He identified a partner to help raise capital and Cumulus was launched in May of 1997. Cumulus went public through an IPO in 1998 and Dickey, who spent the first two years building the platform through multiple acquisitions, became Chairman & CEO in 2000 and served in that capacity for 16 years.

Over 19 years, Dickey built Cumulus into the nation's second largest radio company, growing it to 460 stations in 90 markets and the country's largest radio network, Westwood One with $1.2 billion in revenue and 6,500 employees.

In addition to Cumulus, Dickey is also co-founder and chairman of DM Luxury which acquired Modern Luxury Media in 2010 and built it into the country's largest regional magazine company with 68 magazines in the top 20 luxury markets including titles: *Manhattan, Angeleno, Chicago Social, San Francisco, Silicon Valley, Dallas, DC, Houston, Atlantan, Miami, San Diego, Scottsdale and Aspen* magazines.

Dickey holds a Bachelor's and Master's degrees in English Literature from Stanford University and an MBA from Harvard Business School. Dickey has been named Executive of the Year by *Radio Ink* magazine, and Broadcasting CEO of the Year by *Institutional Investor* magazine. He is also the author of *The Franchise – Building Radio Brands*, recognized as a definitive text on radio competition and strategy.

INDEX